Praise for *WE'RE ALL IN THIS TOGETHER*

"Creating a healthy team and a strong culture are essential competitive advantages in today's business world. Mike Robbins shares tangible techniques that leaders and teams can use to excel, backs up his ideas with important research, and provides a road map for creating a team environment of personal connection and optimal performance."

— **Tom Rath**, *New York Times* best-selling co-author of *How Full is Your Bucket?*

"Great teams embrace conflict and inclusion. What a powerful paradox. I love this book as an inspiration every day to self-reflect on our culture. It's not a coincidence that the rallying cry for our customers is '*All Together Now*,' as we try to integrate siloed IT teams with our products. Teamwork is compelling business."

— **Dheeraj Pandey**, CEO of Nutanix

"Building and sustaining a team that loves working together takes courage, commitment, and a willingness to be radically candid. The tools Mike Robbins offers in *We're All in This Together* give you and your team the skills you need to love your work—and working together."

— **Kim Scott**, *New York Times* best-selling author of *Radical Candor*

"Mike Robbins has been a great partner for me and our team at Deltek. The important ideas he shares in *We're All in This Together* have had a positive impact on our team, our customers, and our culture."

— **Mike Corkery**, President and CEO of Deltek

"I've been friends with Mike Robbins since we were teammates at Stanford. Whether it's in baseball, business, or life, he knows what it means to be a true champion. *We're All in This Together* is a book that will help you and your team come together and perform at the highest level."

— **Brodie Van Wagenen**, Executive Vice President and General Manager of the New York Mets

"The powerful ideas that Mike Robbins shares in *We're All in This Together* have inspired me and my team at the NBA. This book can help unlock the greatness in your team by teaching you specific tools for authentic connection, giving and receiving essential feedback, and challenging each other in a way that brings out the best in everyone."

— **Amy Brooks**, President, Team Marketing and Business Operations and Chief Innovation Officer of the NBA

"Great leaders, teams, and organizations know that culture is a fundamental competitive advantage. In *We're All in This Together*, Mike Robbins gives you and your team ways to build trust and an authentic sense of belonging."

— **Chip Conley**, author of *Wisdom@Work* and Strategic Advisor for Hospitality & Leadership at Airbnb

"Working with Mike Robbins over the past decade has been a catalyst for the growth and success of our culture and our business. The concepts he teaches in *We're All in This Together* have had a profound impact on me, our leaders, and our entire company."

— **Jason Hughes**, Chairman, CEO, and Owner of Hughes Marino

"For leaders, teams, and organizations to thrive in today's diverse business world, it's essential to actively create an environment where everyone is included and knows that they belong. *We're All in This Together* is a catalyst for creating and enhancing this type of culture within your team and company."

— **Jennifer Brown**, author of *How to Be an Inclusive Leader*

"In sports, business, and life, teamwork is fundamental to success. In *We're All in This Together*, Mike Robbins teaches us important techniques for how to come together, find common ground, and create a thriving team culture of high performance."

— **Andre Chambers**, Vice President of People Operations for the Oakland A's

"I've had the honor of working with high-performing teams in many different industries over the past two decades. The insights, techniques, and practices Mike Robbins shares in *We're All in This Together* will make your team great. I highly recommend this book!"

— **Jon Gordon**, *Wall Street Journal* best-selling author of *The Power of a Positive Team*

"I've known Mike Robbins for many years. His approach and ideas have had a powerful impact on me and my team. *We're All in This Together* is an important book that will help you, your team, and your organization be your best."

— **Keith White**, Executive Vice President of Loss Prevention at Gap Inc.

"Creating a culture of belonging is one of the most impactful actions leaders can take to create a high-performing team. In *We're All in This Together*, Mike Robbins shows us how to do this and gives us specific techniques for making it happen."

— **Eric Severson**, EVP and Chief People Office at Neiman Marcus Group

"What Mike Robbins teaches us is that having the courage to be vulnerable is necessary for teams to trust each other, collaborate, and perform at a high level. In his latest work, *We're All in This Together*, he inspires us to connect with each other authentically and create the psychological safety our teams need to thrive."

— **Aditi Dhagat**, VP and Fellow, Marketing Technologies at Intuit

"I've had a chance to travel throughout the world and meet people from so many different countries, companies, and cultures. As Mike Robbins addresses in *We're All in This Together*, we are all way more alike than we are different. Teams, organizations, and communities who understand and embody this are the most healthy and successful."

— **Gopi Kallayil**, Chief Evangelist of Brand Marketing at Google and author of *The Happy Human*

"Mike Robbins reminds us about the importance of embracing vulnerability, that we're much more than the masks we wear, and that we often have more in common than we think. *We're All in This Together* is a powerful call to action for us to come together and support each other."

— **Ashanti Branch**, Founder and Executive Director of the Ever Forward Club

WE'RE ALL IN THIS TOGETHER

Also by Mike Robbins

Books

Be Yourself, Everyone Else Is Already Taken: Transform Your Life with the Power of Authenticity

Bring Your Whole Self to Work: How Vulnerability Unlocks Creativity, Connection, and Performance*

Focus on the Good Stuff: The Power of Appreciation

Nothing Changes Until You Do: A Guide to Self-Compassion and Getting Out of Your Own Way*

CDs

The Power of Appreciation

*Available from Hay House

Please visit:

Hay House USA: www.hayhouse.com®
Hay House Australia: www.hayhouse.com.au
Hay House UK: www.hayhouse.co.uk
Hay House India: www.hayhouse.co.in

WE'RE ALL IN THIS TOGETHER

Creating a
Team Culture of
High Performance,
Trust, and Belonging

MIKE ROBBINS

HAY HOUSE, INC.
Carlsbad, California • New York City
London • Sydney • New Delhi

Published in the United States by: Hay House, Inc.: www.hayhouse.com®
Published in Australia by: Hay House Australia Pty. Ltd.: www.hayhouse.com.au
Published in the United Kingdom by: Hay House UK, Ltd.: www.hayhouse.co.uk
Published in India by: Hay House Publishers India: www.hayhouse.co.in

Cover design: Brad Foltz
Interior design: Bryn Starr Best

Cataloging-in-Publication Data is on file at the Library of Congress.

Hardcover ISBN: 978-1-4019-5813-8

E-book ISBN: 978-1-4019-5814-5

Audiobook ISBN: 978-1-4019-5815-2

10 9 8 7 6 5 4 3 2 1
1st edition, May 2020

Printed in the United States of America

Michelle, Samantha, and Rosie:
You are my most important team,
and I love you very much. Thank you for
being you, and for all of your love, compassion,
and support. I'm glad we're all in this
beautiful family together!

CONTENTS

Introduction xi

Pillar #1: Create Psychological Safety 1

Pillar #2: Focus on Inclusion and Belonging 39

Pillar #3: Embrace Sweaty-Palmed Conversations . . . 81

Pillar #4: Care About and Challenge Each Other . . . 123

Conclusion 161

Resources 165

Acknowledgments 169

About the Author 173

INTRODUCTION

My first real awareness of the importance and impact of team dynamics came during my third season of Little League Baseball in 1985. I was 11 years old that summer. We got off to a hot start—winning our first four games, which was more than we had won in either of the previous two years. Getting off to that 4–0 start was exciting. Alex, our other pitcher, and I were pretty dominant and we had some real confidence. As a team, we also knew each other quite well, liked one another a lot, and seemed to really be rooting for everyone to succeed. Winning is, of course, much more fun than losing, and we liked it.

But then we lost our fifth game, pretty badly, and then our sixth one also. We didn't respond all that well to losing—there was lots of whining, finger-pointing, and arguing. Our coach, David, was frustrated with us but didn't really know what to do. Since I'd been on the team for a few years and was one of the best players, I found myself in a new and unique situation—essentially being the captain. David suggested that I call a player's only meeting to talk to the team about what was going on. Although I didn't quite know what to say or how to do it, I agreed.

I called the team down the right field line and we sat in a circle on the grass.

"We're much better than how we've played these last two games. And, I don't think us arguing and blaming each other is going to help us start winning again," I said.

We sat on that field and had a conversation for quite a while about our team and what we needed to do to get ourselves back on track. Toward the end of the discussion, my teammate Sam spoke up for the first time and said, "We gotta play harder and give it everything we have—110 percent!" Something about what Sam said and the passion with which he said it really resonated with me and a bunch of the other kids on our team. Our heads were nodding, and many of us were saying, "Yes!"

From then on, we took on the mantra of "110," which was code for *Give it everything you've got*. We started saying that to each other at our next practice, "110," and during our next game, "110," which we won. We ended up winning the rest of our games in the regular season, finished 8–2, and took first place in our division, which meant we qualified for the playoffs and would have a chance to play for the city championship, which was a new and exciting experience for us.

We played well in the playoffs, although we didn't end up winning the city title. However, that whole experience of starting the season well, struggling in the middle, coming together as a team, and then turning things around really had an impact on me. What made that team special and allowed us to be successful was the way we worked together, challenged each other, and supported one another. We had some pretty good players, but it was our *teamwork* that made the difference. Not only were many of us friends in school, we were also personally invested in each other's success. And, we were willing to push ourselves and everyone else on the team to give it everything we had (110 percent).

Yes, it was just Little League Baseball and I was only 11, but it was the first of many experiences I've had in my life where the dynamics of the team, the relationships among the members, and the way everyone came together had a *huge* impact on the ultimate success of the group.

Have you ever been a part of a team or leading a team where the talent was strong but the team didn't perform that well? Most of us have had this experience. On the flip side, have you ever been on a team that may not have had a group of rock stars in terms of pure talent, but something about the team just *worked*, and the group really performed well together? Most of us have had this experience as well. I've been fascinated by this phenomenon ever since my Little League experience as a kid.

As you may know, I continued to play baseball and got drafted by the New York Yankees out of high school. I didn't sign a contract with them at that time, because I got an opportunity to play baseball at Stanford University. Although my childhood dream was to play in the major leagues, I chose to go to Stanford because of the high quality of education I would receive and the incredible success of the university's baseball team. Ultimately, I signed with the Kansas City Royals, who drafted me in 1995 out of Stanford.

When you sign a contract with a major league team like the Royals, or the Yankees, Giants, Cubs, or any other pro baseball team in North America, you first go into the minor leagues. There are six different levels in the minors to make your way through before you get to the majors. Unfortunately for me, during my third season in the minors, I tore ligaments in my pitching elbow. Two years and three surgeries later, I was forced to retire from baseball.

As devastated as I was when my baseball career ended— and I *was*—and as much as I loved the game—and I *did*—my fascination with the impact of team dynamics on success continued to grow and expand. Some of the teams I was on had really talented players, but we didn't perform all that well. It didn't make sense to me. In sports, if you have good players you should have a good team, right? Not always. Yet there were other teams I was on where the talent was decent, not great, but the team was fantastic. We would sometimes beat other teams with better players, which I found both confusing and intriguing.

How was this possible? I wasn't completely sure at the time, but we did talk about it a bit among ourselves. We called it "team chemistry," and though no one could quite define what it was exactly, we knew when we had it, and we definitely knew when we *didn't*. And it wasn't just some warm, fuzzy, touchy-feely thing; it actually made a big difference in terms of how we performed. The teams with good chemistry played much better than the ones without it. And, for me as an individual, it was always easier to succeed personally when the chemistry of the team was strong.

After my baseball career ended in the late '90s, I moved back home to the San Francisco Bay Area and got a job working for a tech company. I assumed the business world would be really different than the sports world, and it was. However, not long into my first job working in online ad sales I realized that the whole team chemistry thing, which I'd erroneously thought was a sports thing, was not exclusive to sports. Deep down, it's really about groups of human beings and how they work with one another. In business, we call it *culture,* and it's made up of those intangible factors of a team that either bring them together or push them apart, as well as the quality of the relationships and the collective sense of the group. In other words, it's how we feel about ourselves on the team, how we relate to our teammates, and how we feel about the group and what we're doing as a whole. As I'm sure you've experienced in your life and career, culture has a huge impact on the success or failure of any team or business. One of my favorite quotes about this, attributed to the late, great leadership guru Peter Drucker, is "Culture eats strategy for breakfast."

After working for two different Internet companies in the late '90s, I ultimately got laid off when the dot-com bubble burst in 2000. However, I'd become so curious about the impact and dynamics of team culture by then, I decided to start my own consulting business and to focus my attention and my work on this full time. I wanted to figure out what could be done to create positive environments and true success for people, leaders, teams, and organizations. Why did some groups thrive while others struggled? It seemed to be more about these intangible qualities and less about the talent and skill of those involved.

For the past 20 years, this is what I've been studying, researching, speaking, and writing about. I've had a chance to travel around the United States and the world, talking to and working with all different types of individuals, groups, and companies. I've been honored to partner with organizations like Google, Wells Fargo, Microsoft, Schwab, eBay, Genentech, Gap, the NBA, the Oakland A's, and so many others—helping them enhance the culture and performance of their teams. In addition to these large, well-known brands, I've also worked with small businesses, government agencies, educational institutions, nonprofits, local school districts, and more. And, while each team and organization have their own unique challenges, goals, and dynamics, there are some universal qualities that allow teams to come together, trust each other, and perform at the highest level.

According to Deloitte's 2016 Global Human Capital Trends report, "There are few factors that contribute more to business success than the system of values, beliefs, and behaviors that shape how real work gets done within an organization." And, 82 percent of the respondents to this survey believe that "culture is a competitive advantage."

Working with so many successful and diverse groups has taught me a lot about what it takes for teams to thrive. It almost always comes down to our ability to connect, align, and create a culture in which we know *we're all in this together.*

The Fierce Urgency of Now

I felt compelled to write this book at this moment in time for two main reasons. First of all, the fifth and final principle of my last book, *Bring Your Whole Self to Work*, is "Create a Championship Team." And while I explored team performance in that chapter, I felt like it was important to double-click on this topic and dive deeper into the specific components that are necessary for great teamwork, as well as the practical steps needed to create a thriving culture. As I've seen through my latest research and by working with teams at every level, organizations of various sizes, and companies in different industries, having a strong culture is both more challenging and more essential than ever these days—especially given the incredibly fast-paced nature of business today, the fact that many groups are distributed across multiple locations, and the global diversity of the workforce.

Second of all, Dr. Martin Luther King Jr. often spoke of the "fierce urgency of now." We are living in fascinating, intense, and challenging times from a cultural perspective—here in the United States and elsewhere. A lot has happened in our country and our world over the past few years that has more deeply divided us along cultural, political, and ideological lines. While this isn't a new phenomenon by any stretch, there is an element of it that has felt different and deeply troubling to me. We see it playing out in the news and our social media feeds every day. And it impacts how we communicate, interact, and work with one another. This book and my work are not about politics or society, per se. However, the way we engage with each other, discuss and debate important issues that we may disagree about, and challenge ourselves to find common ground with one another, especially when we have different beliefs and backgrounds, has *everything* to do with our ability to create a healthy team environment and do great work together. In addition, the current political and cultural climate, as well as the rise of important social movements, has brought more focused awareness to issues of race, gender, inequality, privilege, and more—both at work and in general. We can no longer opt out of addressing these things, even though they can often be confusing, uncomfortable, and difficult. How we think about these issues and deal with them in our teams and our work is *fundamental* to the overall success of our organizations and our society.

Addressing issues of diversity and inclusion aren't just important societally, they are good for the bottom line of business as well. In 2017, Boston Consulting Group found that companies that have more diverse management teams have 19 percent higher revenue. And, according to a 2018 study conducted by McKinsey & Co., racially and ethnically diverse organizations outperform industry norms by 33 percent.

Our Very First Team

For most of us, myself included, our family is our very first team. It's the group of people we're born into that informs how we engage with and look at the world. The health, size, and overall dynamics of our family of origin also have a huge impact on us as we grow and evolve. My family situation, like so many others, was complicated and challenging. It affected how I interacted with other people and how I engaged on teams and within groups specifically, as it does for most of us.

I was born in Oakland, California, in 1974. My parents both came from the East Coast—my dad was Jewish and grew up in Hartford, Connecticut; my mom was Irish Catholic and grew up in the small town of Westerly, Rhode Island. They met in San Francisco in the late 1960s, got married, moved to Oakland, had my sister Lori and then me, four years later. They split up when I was three years old. Mom raised Lori and me basically by herself as my Dad suffered from bipolar disorder, and by the time I was about seven, he had lost his job in radio and spiraled down over the next few years. He was in and out of our lives and mental institutions and not able to contribute to our family financially, emotionally, or practically. It was painful, confusing, and sad for me to grow up without my father around. And while I came to more fully understand and have empathy for his mental illness as I got older, when I was a kid it didn't make sense to me; all I knew was that my dad wasn't around much, couldn't work, and had some kind of strange condition that made him feel sad, angry, and unmotivated most of the time. My mom did the best she could but struggled in many ways raising us on her own.

I did feel loved and supported, especially by my mom and Lori, but there was a lot of pain and sadness, as well as shame and embarrassment given the situation with my dad, as well as our lack of money, which manifested in the relatively poor condition of our house, car, and other things. In addition, just about all of our extended family members on both sides lived far away, so we were isolated and forced to deal with these challenges on our own. As is the case in many families, especially when divorce happens, there were lots of unresolved resentments and unspoken expectations among various relatives on both sides, along with a significant lack of communication, understanding, and support.

My nuclear family was essentially a very small "team," isolated from our larger team (the extended family), with limited resources, and dealing with some significant challenges. Yet even with all of this going on, I was still a pretty happy kid. However, I found myself longing for deeper connections and wanting to be part of something bigger—a larger group of people, a thriving community, and a healthier environment. It was this desire, in part, that drew me to sports and other group activities. Playing baseball and basketball, being involved in student government, Boy Scouts, the school newspaper, the yearbook, and various clubs all made me feel like I belonged to something bigger than myself, and I loved that. These diverse groups and teams had more people, additional resources, and provided opportunities for me to learn, grow, succeed, and connect with others from different families and backgrounds.

We each learn a lot from our very first team—our family. Regardless of how wonderful or challenging our family situation is, it gives us the initial lens we use to see the world and the framework for how we think about working with others.

Based on all that I learned through my family situation, as well as growing up in the incredibly diverse city of Oakland, going to Stanford, playing competitive sports for 18 years, working for two different tech companies, and now working with teams of all kinds in the business world over the past 20 years, I've come to realize some simple yet profound things when it comes to teamwork. We're all unique, which is important for us to try to understand, acknowledge, and appreciate as best as we possibly can, especially in today's world. And, paradoxically, at the very same time we're way more alike than we are different. Great teams figure out how to harness the positive power of their collective talent, perspective, skills, and personalities— even and especially if they may be different. However, this is often easier said than done. As important as teamwork is, it can also be incredibly difficult.

Five Reasons Teamwork Is Challenging

Although most of us think of teamwork as a positive thing, and our desire for healthy and productive collaboration is real, it's important for us to acknowledge some of the key things (in addition to any baggage we bring from our family of origin) that make working in a team challenging. According to a study conducted by

Salesforce, 86 percent of employees and executives cite lack of collaboration or ineffective communication for workplace failures.

Here are the five biggest things that make it difficult for us to work with others effectively and create a productive team environment:

1. We aren't trained to work in teams. Most of us didn't receive much helpful or healthy teamwork training growing up. Many, like me, had challenging family environments filled with varying degrees of pain and dysfunction. Even if we come from a really healthy family, played team sports, or were involved in other team-oriented activities, our primary training for work comes through school. And, what was "teamwork" called when we were in school?

Cheating!

We were encouraged to do our own work, and we were graded *individually* on how we performed on tests, papers, and projects. Group projects in school were few and far between, and often the experience of doing them was frustrating because it was hard to get everyone on the same page and to make sure they all did their fair share of the work.

And yet after years of education that often *discourages* teamwork, many of us find ourselves in the business world being told to work within a team. Although some organizations encourage teamwork more than others, we still tend to get evaluated, compensated, and promoted as individuals, so the incentive or motivation to work collaboratively is often undercut.

2. We get caught in the trap of "Us versus Them." There are so many examples of the "Us versus Them" trap in our society today—along political, religious, cultural, racial, and other lines. And while these are often overt and upsetting for many reasons, it's sometimes the subtler ones that can be more insidious, especially inside organizations. I see this all the time with the companies I work with. It's the engineering team vs. the sales team, or the HR team vs. the legal team, or the San Francisco office vs. the New York office, and so on. We separate ourselves, compete with each other in negative ways, and defend our positions. In some cases, these divides are almost encouraged by the leaders, the structure, or the mentality of the organization—based on how the company operates, how people are paid, or the nature of recognition, communication, and expectations.

On a human level, this is often driven by our significant need to belong to a tight-knit and specific group. We want to belong so much so that we identify with our role, level, function, office, region, or some other subset of the company to our own detriment. In essence, we forget that we're all part of the same larger team.

3. We focus too much on mechanics. I heard peak-performance expert Tony Robbins speak many years ago, and it had a big impact on my thinking. Tony said that, in almost every circumstance, "80 percent of success is due to psychology—mindset, beliefs, and emotions—and only 20 percent is due to mechanics—the specific steps needed to accomplish a result." Through my own experiences in sports and business, as well as my research on performance and success, I have found this to be true—both for individuals and teams. The challenge is that we spend so much of our time, energy, and attention focused on the mechanics that we sometimes forget to address the psychology, which diminishes our ability to be successful.

From a team standpoint, I often describe mechanics as "above the line" (what we do and how we do it) and psychology as "below the line" (how we think and feel, our perspective, and the overall morale and culture of the group). Since the below-the-line stuff leads to 80 percent of our success as a team, we have to pay more attention to these intangibles and be less obsessed with the mechanics. How open we are with each other, how much we trust one another, our level of appreciation, and the attitude of our group are some of the important below-the-line things that we can focus on as a team to help us truly succeed.

4. We're often separated by time and space. One significant consequence of today's global workforce and the advancements in technology that allow us to work from anywhere is that we're often separated by time and space. Many of the companies I work with have offices throughout the U.S. and around the world, which is amazing but also poses a myriad of logistical, relational, and cultural challenges. Even for smaller companies that may have fewer employees or who all work in the same location, people sometimes work from home and we often find ourselves doing business with people in other parts of the country or the world.

Basic things like times of calls or meetings, platforms of communication, and styles of working come into play and can create difficulty. Sometimes language and cultural differences play a role in our ability to connect and collaborate effectively. And there are many nonverbal and emotional aspects of our relationships and communication that we miss when we aren't sitting in the same room, looking in each other's eyes, reading body language, and spending time with one another face-to-face.

5. We're focused on ourselves. Even though we all want to belong, and we do care about others, let's face it: Most of us are self-interested, especially at work. This doesn't necessarily mean that we're selfish, it simply means that we're looking out for ourselves and our own interests. Given the nature of the global economy, the volatility we've seen over the past two decades in the job market, and the way we approach our careers today, there are lots of good reasons we tend to focus on ourselves professionally. When we do this, however, we aren't as plugged into what's going on for the people around us, don't put as much attention on the success of the team as we could, and sometimes worry (consciously or unconsciously) that if we pay too much attention to others and the team, it might have a negative impact on us and our career. While this is common and understandable, ultimately it makes partnering, collaborating, and teaming with others more difficult. Ironically, even if we don't really care at all about the success of those around us, it's actually in our best personal interest to be a good team player. Why? Because when we're on a team that does well, it almost always benefits us personally. And when we're on a team that struggles, it almost always impacts us negatively.

The paradox of teamwork is that for us to fully show up, engage, be successful, and create meaning and fulfillment in our work, collaborating with others is essential; yet, at the same time, there are forces within us (like our egos, personal ambitions, and fears) and within our teams and organizations (like negative competition, territorialism, and scarcity), that can spur us to focus primarily on ourselves. It's important for us to acknowledge these and other challenges with ownership and compassion, and to work through them as best we can. Teamwork can be difficult, and often involves lots of growth opportunities for us and our colleagues. However, the benefits of healthy collaboration are so great, we must have the awareness and courage to move beyond these challenges, even if they're significant. Doing this allows us to create the type of culture that we truly want—one that supports the success of the team and everyone involved.

The intention of this book is to help you break down the barriers of whatever may get in your way—personally, organizationally, and culturally—so that you and your team can connect more deeply with one another, trust each other, and perform at the highest level. It can be a catalyst that takes you and your team from where you are right now to where you truly want to be. And, on a deeper level, it's about reminding you and everyone around you that there really isn't a "them," it's all us.

About This Book

This book offers you specific insights, ideas, tools, and techniques that you can incorporate into how you work and lead, which will allow you to be even more successful and effective. I wrote this book specifically for teams, so you can read it along with the people you work with as a way to create, enhance, and deepen your culture of high performance, trust, and belonging, thus allowing you and your team to be the absolute best you can be.

Throughout the book, I share stories from my personal and professional life. I also share examples from the people I've interviewed on my podcast and from the companies I've worked with over the years. Additionally, you'll get some of the latest data and research on these important topics, along with ideas, techniques, and best practices I've learned from various experts, clients, and others.

The book is organized into four key pillars:

Pillar 1. Create Psychological Safety. Psychological safety is a shared belief that the team is safe for risk-taking. People on teams with psychological safety have a sense of confidence that their team will not embarrass, reject, or punish them for speaking up or taking risks. The team climate is characterized by an atmosphere of interpersonal trust and mutual respect in which people are comfortable being themselves without fear of negative consequences to their self-image, status, or career. Essentially, psychological safety is trust at a group level.

Harvard Business School professor Amy Edmondson has researched and written extensively about psychological safety over the past 20 years. "It's not enough for organizations to simply hire talent," she says. "If leaders want to unleash individual and collective talent, they must foster a psychologically safe climate where employees feel free to contribute ideas, share information, and report mistakes."

A 2017 Gallup study found that only three in ten employees strongly agree with the statement that their opinions count at work. Gallup calculated that by "moving the ratio to six in ten employees, organizations could realize a 27 percent reduction in turnover, a 40 percent reduction in safety incidents, and a 12 percent increase in productivity."

Pillar 2. Focus on Inclusion and Belonging. An essential element of creating a safe environment that allows people to trust each other, collaborate with one another, and perform at their highest level as a team is inclusion and belonging. There are countless studies linking inclusion to higher profits, increased engagement scores, and enhanced business results.

For example, according to a study of 140 U.S. companies by Accenture alongside the American Association of People with Disabilities and Disability:IN, those that offered the most inclusive working environment for employees with disabilities achieved an average 28 percent higher revenue, 30 percent greater economic profit margins, and twice the net income of their industry peers between 2015 and 2018.

Inclusion means "having respect for and appreciation of differences in ethnicity, gender, age, national origin, disability, sexual orientation, education, and religion." It also means "actively involving everyone's ideas, knowledge, perspectives, approaches, and styles to maximize business success." And, as important as it is for us to focus on both diversity and inclusion, the ultimate goal is to create an environment on the team and in the company where everyone feels as though they belong, regardless of who they are, the role they have, and their background.

Pillar 3. Embrace Sweaty-Palmed Conversations. Great teams embrace conflict and feedback as natural and important aspects of growth, collaboration, and success. This means we have to be willing to have those awkward, uncomfortable, sweaty-palmed conversations with each other. The problem is that because conflict and feedback can be hard, most teams aren't very good at it. However, when team members create an environment that is conducive to having healthy and productive conflict, they have an ability to connect more deeply, navigate challenges effectively, give each other feedback in a way that makes everyone better, and innovate in ways that allow them to thrive.

Research conducted by CPP Inc., publisher of the Myers-Briggs Type Indicator, has shown that in the U.S., workplace conflict costs companies more than $350 billion a year. And that figure reflects just the time people spend dealing with conflict; it doesn't include the emotional, psychological, and physical toll it takes on people personally.

Nate Regier, author of *Conflict without Casualties*, whom I had a chance to interview on my podcast, says, "The purpose of conflict is to create, not destroy."

Pillar 4. Care About and Challenge Each Other. What I've seen, experienced, and learned about high-performing teams over the years is that they understand and have a balance of two important things at the same time: *Caring About Each Other* and *Challenging Each Other*. Both are essential and both have to be focused on with the same level of intensity for the team and all of its members to perform at the highest level.

For a team to thrive there must be a deep level of trust that everyone has each other's backs, has good intentions, and is moving in the same direction together.

In a piece published in the *Harvard Business Review* in 2017, neuroeconomist Paul Zak writes, "Compared with people at low-trust companies, people at high-trust companies report 74 percent less stress, 50 percent higher productivity, and 76 percent more engagement." In other words, creating a strong culture of trust, as well as an environment where people know they're cared about and supported by their teammates, leads to significantly greater engagement and performance.

In every chapter of this book, I explore what each of these important pillars are, why they can be challenging, and how to implement them successfully into how you work, lead, and create team culture. I'm excited and honored that you've chosen to join me on this journey. I hope you and your team find it useful, enlightening, and empowering.

Here we go . . .

CREATE PSYCHOLOGICAL SAFETY

In 2015 the Golden State Warriors had a magical season and won their first NBA championship in 40 years. As a lifelong Warriors fan, this was very exciting to me, especially since for much of those 40 years, the Warriors were one of the worst teams in the NBA.

Their journey to that title in 2015 involved a pivotal moment during the NBA Finals that exemplified the importance of psychological safety, which is what this first pillar is all about, and is a foundational aspect of creating a team culture of high performance, trust, and belonging.

During the previous two seasons, the Warriors had played well and made the playoffs but got knocked out in the second and first rounds respectively. In 2015, under first-year head coach Steve Kerr, they made their way through all three rounds of the playoffs and ended up in the NBA Finals. They were matched up against LeBron James and the Cleveland Cavaliers. Not only was James the best player in the league, he was playing in his sixth NBA Finals—and fifth in a row. None of the Warriors' key players had ever been to the Finals before.

In those first few games under the bright lights, the Warriors seemed a bit rattled and overmatched. They lost Game 3 in Cleveland, to go down 2–1 in the series. The

Cavs had seized the momentum and were forcing the Warriors to play at their slower pace, which greatly benefited Cleveland.

Nick U'Ren, a 28-year-old special assistant to Steve Kerr, pored over the film from Game 3 and did a ton of research before Game 4, trying to figure out what the Warriors could do to alter the dynamic of the series. He suggested making a significant change to the starting lineup—replacing the Warriors' seven-foot center Andrew Bogut with the much smaller Andre Iguodala, a six-foot-eight-inch swingman.

Iguodala had been coming off the bench for the Warriors all season, even though he had spent his entire career as a very successful starter. Putting him in the starting lineup would mean that Warriors forward Draymond Green, who was also six-foot-eight, would move to center. Although Draymond was their passionate, vocal leader on the court putting him in that position at his size would put a lot of pressure on him and was a risky move for them to make at the time.

Cleveland jumped to a 7–0 lead early in Game 4, but Kerr saw that the smaller lineup was creating the space that the Warriors' shooters needed and was allowing them to accelerate the tempo of the game, which played to their strengths. Kerr stuck with this smaller unit, and the Warriors tied the series that night with an impressive 103–82 Game 4 victory. They won the next two games as Cleveland frantically tried to counter the adjustment but couldn't.

The Warriors won that historic championship and went on to have one of the greatest five-year runs in the history of sports, which included two more titles and five straight trips to Finals. Andre Iguodala played so well that even though he didn't start those first three games, he was still named the MVP of the 2015 NBA Finals.

There are many reasons why the Warriors were able to win that championship in 2015 and go on their incredible run of success. Of course, talent, luck, execution, hard work, timing, commitment, and the incredible team chemistry they established all played significant roles.

And Steve Kerr created an environment with his coaching staff and his players where everyone was empowered to speak up, offer ideas, and even make bold suggestions like changing the starting lineup in the middle of the NBA Finals. Nick U'Ren was a junior member of the coaching staff, but he was given the opportunity to offer up an idea that changed the trajectory of that series. He felt safe enough, even in his lower-level role, to make a risky suggestion to the person in charge. And, not only was his idea listened to, it was implemented in a way that had a significant impact on the outcome of the series.

Kerr said publicly after Game 4 that if the lineup change hadn't have worked, he would have taken full responsibility for it as the leader. But, when it paid off the way that it did, he praised U'Ren, gave him credit publicly for suggesting it, and acknowledged his players for embracing the change and executing on it.

The coaching staff and the players of the Golden State Warriors knew they had the psychological safety to speak up, try new things, take risks, be themselves, and even fail—in service of their growth, development, and success. When leaders and teams courageously work to create this kind of atmosphere, they can produce extraordinary results together.

What Is Psychological Safety?

The concept of psychological safety was popularized by researcher and Harvard Business School professor Amy Edmondson. According to her research, and as I mentioned in the Introduction, it is a shared belief that the team is safe for risk-taking. People on teams with psychological safety know that their leader and fellow team members will not embarrass, reject, or punish them for speaking up, disagreeing, making mistakes, being bold, or even failing. The team intentionally creates an atmosphere of interpersonal trust and mutual respect in which people are comfortable being exactly who they are—without worrying about damage to their self-image, status, or career.

Psychological safety is not quite the same as trust, however; it focuses on a belief that we have about our group, while trust focuses on a belief that we have about someone else in particular. Furthermore, psychological safety is defined by how we think we're viewed by others on the team, whereas trust is defined by how we view another or we think they view us. In other words, trust is a one-on-one phenomenon, whereas psychological safety is a group phenomenon. When we're talking about psychological safety, we're essentially talking about group trust. Psychological safety is foundational to our human need for belonging, which we will focus on specifically in Pillar #2. It's the core building block for teamwork, collaboration, and performance.

Google conducted an in-depth research project a few years ago aimed at determining the key factors that consistently produce high-performing teams. "Project Aristotle," as it was called, involved gathering and assessing data from 180 teams across Google, as well as looking at key studies in the fields of organizational psychology and team effectiveness. Analysis of the research data revealed a number of key findings.

First and foremost, it seems that *who* is on a team matters a bit less than *how* the team members interact, structure their work, and view their contributions.

Secondly, the findings identified five key traits that set successful teams apart:

1. **Psychological safety:** Can we take risks on this team without feeling insecure or embarrassed?

2. **Dependability:** Can we count on each other to do high-quality work on time?

3. **Structure and clarity:** Are the team's goals, roles, and execution plans clear?

4. **Meaning of work:** Are we working on something that is important for each of us personally?

5. **Impact of work:** Do we fundamentally believe that the work we're doing matters?

Third, according to Project Aristotle, psychological safety was far and away the most important of the five elements—the underpinning of the other four.

When I talked to Karen May, vice president of people development at Google during the time these findings were released, she said, "We weren't surprised to learn that psychological safety was important to the success of teams, but we were amazed to find out *how significantly important* it was."

Taking a risk around our team members might seem simple, but it takes a lot of courage. We're usually willing to do it only if we know there won't be harsh retribution or that we won't get kicked out of the group for doing so.

Most of us are reluctant to engage in behaviors that could negatively influence how others perceive our competence, personality, or intelligence. Although this kind of self-protection is a natural instinct in the workplace, it's often detrimental to effective teamwork. The safer we feel with those on our team, the more likely we'll be to take risks, admit mistakes, partner with others, and take on new roles and challenges.

Google's study showed that individual performance and approach were also impacted by psychological safety. People on teams with higher psychological safety are less likely to leave, more likely to harness the power of diverse ideas from their teammates, bring in more revenue, and are rated as effective twice as often by executives.

I've seen the importance of psychological safety up close for many years with the teams and leaders I coach. When a team creates standards, rituals, and practices, both explicitly and implicitly, that allow their members to be themselves, speak up, make mistakes, debate in healthy ways, and even fail, they're more likely to trust each other, collaborate with one another effectively, and succeed as a team.

I was working with the executive leadership team of a financial services company a few years ago. The team was made up of really smart, talented leaders, but the company had gone through a number of changes and they weren't performing at an optimal level. The CEO, let's call him Chris, was fairly new in his role and the team was made up of some folks who had been there for a while and a few others who had come on board more recently. They were working very hard to turn things around for the company, yet they were facing significant challenges. The team got along fairly well, but they were frustrated with the lack of results, seemed to be feeling a lot of pressure, and had very different ideas about what was needed to get the organization moving in the right direction. There was also a bit of a divide between the people who had been there for a while and those who were newer to the team.

Chris said he wanted the team members to have open and honest discussions about some of the core issues they were facing, but he got very uncomfortable when there was conflict and also got quite defensive when people challenged him. He was demonstratively frustrated by their lackluster performance, and he talked about it a lot—calling people out and complaining that they weren't meeting their goals. This put people on edge, shut down most attempts at healthy debate, and made it hard for the leaders on this team to engage in a genuine and productive way.

I spent time connecting with each of the members of the team on the phone prior to our initial in-person group session and got some specific insight and perspective from them individually about their primary challenges and team dynamics. However, when we got together the first time, it was obvious to me that our phone conversations were very different from the conversation we were having together in the room where they didn't seem to feel safe enough to speak up and to address what was going on in an authentic way.

Over the course of the next few months, as I worked with them individually, they were more than willing to express to me their frustration with one another, to admit their fears, and to acknowledge their challenges, but they had a much harder time doing so with each other directly and together as a group. There was a lot of posturing, positioning, and saying things they thought Chris wanted to hear and that would protect them from potential harm, ridicule, or failure.

It took some time, quite a bit of effort, and a lot of courage on their part, but eventually through our work together they began to open up more with one another and to address things more directly as a group. Chris became a bit more willing to embrace healthy debate, and the team began to have conversations as a group that previously they had only with me. In doing this, they were able to build more psychological safety, which allowed them to communicate more openly, collaborate with one another, and align as a leadership team as they made their way through the challenges they were facing. This process was difficult, at times a bit messy, and took continued engagement and commitment by Chris and the entire team.

All the talent and skill in the world can't make up for a lack of psychological safety. It takes real dedication and isn't easy to create or maintain, yet it is so important for the success of your team.

What Makes Psychological Safety Challenging?

To create more psychological safety for your team and in your organization, it's important to acknowledge and understand some of the specific issues and dynamics that make it difficult to foster. Here are some of the things I've seen over the years that get in the way of teams being able to create psychological safety effectively.

• **Fear of Judgment, Criticism, Retribution, or Social Exclusion.** Being judged or criticized can be painful. Most of us have had this happen many times throughout our lives and careers. It doesn't feel good and often shuts us down. When we're part of a team where people are overtly or covertly judged for taking risks, doing things differently, or making mistakes, we're more likely to hold back and be protective. When we see specific examples of retribution or social exclusion for speaking up, expressing vulnerability, and being ourselves, we often make sure to watch our back and play it safe.

When I work with a team whose leader always has to be right or get the final word on key ideas and decisions, or when the team members are judgmental and critical of each other, it puts everyone on edge. When team members spend too much time and energy protecting themselves from one another or even trying to impress each other, it takes away from them connecting, collaborating, and doing great work together.

• **Negative Competition.** Competition is a normal aspect of life, especially in business, but it can be both positive and negative. Positive competition is when we compete against others in a way that brings out the best in everyone involved. Negative competition is when we compete in a win-at-all-costs kind of way. Negative competition has us root against those around us, focus primarily on ourselves, and actively hold people back so that we can get ahead. When a team engages in negative competition, it doesn't feel safe for us to take risks, ask for help, or admit mistakes because we fear these things will be exploited, taken advantage of, and used against us by those on our team.

Back when I played baseball, I was on some teams where people actively rooted against each other, which made it very difficult for us to be successful individually and collectively. Negative competition is often based on fear and scarcity—the notion that there isn't enough to go around. When we're in an environment with lots of negative competition, it makes it hard to trust the people around us or to feel safe on the team, because we know people are ready to pounce on any and every mistake we make to their advantage.

• **Pride and Stubbornness.** Our egos often get in our way. We like to look good, sound smart, do the right thing, solve problems, and produce results. None of these things are all that problematic in and of themselves; however, when we make a mistake, need some support, or have a dissenting opinion about something, our pride or our stubbornness can sometimes get the best of us. We either don't admit our failure or are too prideful to ask for help. We willfully dig in on our position (whether or not we speak up about it) and refuse to see things differently.

I was placed on a jury a few years ago, which was quite an interesting experience. The trial lasted for just a few days and I was appointed as the foreman, which meant it was my job to facilitate the deliberations and try to help the group come to a verdict. We went around the table in our initial discussion to see where everyone was in terms of the case. Even though I was instructed to let everyone know this was an initial discussion of many we would have, one man on the jury said, "He's not guilty, no way! There's nothing anyone can say in here that will get me to change my mind."

While I appreciated his honesty and clarity, he said it with such harshness and stubbornness that it was actually pretty upsetting to everyone in the room. It took us two days, and finally we ended up with a hung jury, 11–1. All the jurors believed the defendant was guilty, except for this one man. And while he had every right to come to this conclusion, his pride and stubbornness made that experience quite painful, scary, and uncomfortable.

• **Lack of Modeling by Leaders.** If the leaders in our organization don't actively create psychologically safe environments, it can be tricky. Sometimes our own manager or others in leadership positions may talk the talk, but they don't walk the walk. In other words, they say all the right things about the importance of taking risks, speaking up, and admitting mistakes, but they either don't actually do so themselves or when it's done by others they react in such a negative way that it doesn't feel safe for us to engage, communicate, and operate that way.

When a senior leader, like Chris, isn't willing to acknowledge their fear, their mistakes, or they come down harshly on someone who fails, it sends a clear message to the team and the entire organization that these types of behaviors aren't safe. The senior leaders of an organization often set the tone for how people operate and what is deemed acceptable.

• **Perfection Demands.** Perfectionism is sometimes celebrated, but it can be quite dangerous. As my friend psychologist Dr. Robert Holden says, "I've never met a happy perfectionist in my life." When the standard we place on ourselves, others, or the team is perfection, we *always* fall short. Having healthy high standards can be incredibly important to our success and the performance of our team. However, when we expect perfection, which by its nature is impossible, we make it very difficult for people to take risks and make mistakes.

When I interviewed Amy Edmondson on my podcast, she said, "It would be great to be perfect, but there's no such thing." She went on to say, "If leaders don't acknowledge this fact, the default assumption people have is that perfection is expected—anything shy of that will result in the leader being upset and the team member being 'dinged' in some way."

• **Imposter Syndrome**. A simple Google search of "what is imposter syndrome" yields this definition:

The persistent inability to believe that one's success is deserved or has been legitimately achieved as a result of one's own efforts or skills.

This is something that I have experienced throughout my life and continue to see all over the place—especially around high-level leaders and very successful people. While it's totally natural for us to question ourselves, particularly when we're given increased responsibility or opportunity, imposter syndrome often causes us to feel like we have to perform for those around us or justify our position. When we do this and people on our teams do this, genuine safety can't exist. We're too busy proving ourselves to others, and don't feel comfortable enough to admit mistakes, speak our truth, or take a risk that might result in failure.

I was first introduced to imposter syndrome most significantly when I got to Stanford as a freshman. I had a basic but profound realization the first day I walked onto campus: Everyone else had gotten into Stanford too. Not only did I no longer feel special, I immediately began to doubt myself and wonder if I was even good enough to be there. All the people I met seemed so much smarter and more talented than I was.

When we feel this way, we tend to overcompensate to prove that we belong. Imposter syndrome can also cause us to hold ourselves back so that we don't get embarrassed or fail miserably. And when the environment around us is such that lots of people are feeling insecure and overcompensating, it makes it all the more challenging for psychological safety to exist.

• **Workplace Politics.** The politics of our team or the company as a whole often come into play when we're looking at how safe things are psychologically. The more political things are, the less safe we usually feel.

When I work with a team or company where there are lots of internal politics, people often say things to me like, "You can't talk about stuff like that around here," or "You have to know how to play the game in this place." In environments that are fraught with politics, there are lots of unwritten rules about how to act and backchannels of communication that make psychological safety difficult.

• **Race, Gender, Age, Orientation.** We will talk about this in much more depth and detail later on, but our race, gender, age, and orientation can play a significant role in the level of psychological safety that exists in our environment. It can be tricky to discuss these topics in an open and productive way and, understandably, it's often emotional and sensitive. We tend to avoid addressing these issues directly, which can make things *even more* challenging. This dynamic can impact how specific individuals feel on the team, as well as how certain comments or actions are perceived. For example, if a man says something it may be taken very differently than if the same thing is said by a woman.

• **Our Role within the Company.** Our title, level, and specific role can also come into play with respect to the psychological safety of the group and how specific people feel on the team. A comment, question, piece of feedback, suggestion, or admission is often taken very differently by others based on the person who makes it. In other words, if the CEO says it, it's bound to be perceived differently than if an intern, or even a midlevel manager, says the exact same thing.

All of the many things I've mentioned here can make it challenging for us to create and experience psychological safety on our teams and in our organizations. These aren't, however, excuses; they're just realities of life and business that we need to acknowledge. Creating and maintaining psychological safety in our teams is essential and foundational to our success, but it can be hard. As my friend and best-selling author Glennon Doyle likes to remind us, "We can do hard things."

The Importance of Authenticity

For your team to perform at the highest level, it's essential that you operate with authenticity. When leaders, team members, and everyone in the organization makes a commitment to authenticity, the psychological safety increases exponentially. As I've said, psychological safety is the foundation of teamwork and performance, which is why we're addressing it here as Pillar #1. Authenticity is fundamental to psychological safety.

I've written extensively about authenticity in my previous books. In *Bring Your Whole Self to Work* I went into detail about the core principles of authenticity as I now understand them. In our discussion here in this chapter, it's important to reiterate some of these specific ideas and to understand how they relate to psychological safety directly.

The Authenticity Continuum

Over the years of studying authenticity, I've realized that it isn't a fixed or constant thing; it exists on a continuum. There are three main aspects of what I call the Authenticity Continuum—phony, honest, and authentic:

Phony————Honest————Authentic

Phony

We all know what it's like to be around someone who is being phony. We usually don't like it, and we often see it as a character flaw. Understandably, we're skeptical of these people, questioning their authenticity and integrity. And, more painfully, most of us have been deceived by people we believed in. This can create a level of mistrust and cynicism that's hard to shake.

However, an important place for us to inquire into phoniness is within *ourselves*. While it's usually pretty easy to point it out in others, looking at it within ourselves can be a bit harder. Where, when, with whom, and in what situations do we find ourselves being phony? It's usually not malicious. And in most cases, when we're being phony we're either unconscious about it or we justify and

15

rationalize it. This happens a lot in business when we're trying to sell an idea or product, as well as when we worry that our opinion might not be well received.

It's important to acknowledge this side of ourselves. We're not bad for operating in phony ways—it can seem like a necessary part of life and business. As long as we notice when we're being inauthentic, we can make different choices. Authenticity is always a choice, and in some cases not an easy one. But when we show up in phony ways, and we either aren't willing to see it or we blame it on other people or the environment, we give away our power and we make it much more challenging for psychological safety to exist.

People often say things to me like, "I *can't* be authentic with my manager," or "You *can't* be authentic here— that's not how people operate." When I hear these things specifically, it's usually a clear indication that there isn't a high level of psychological safety.

However, my response is often something like, "I understand that it can be hard to be authentic—especially with certain people, in specific situations, and at work in general. But the issue isn't that you *can't*, it's that you *won't*. And maybe choosing not to be authentic is what you believe right now to be the best, most self-preserving choice to make. Just own it as a choice. And, like any other choice we make, it comes with certain consequences."

Phoniness is often a symptom as well as a cause of a lack of psychological safety. When we don't feel safe, we're more likely to be phony. And when we're being phony, we make it less safe for people to be real with us and on the team. It is somewhat of a chicken-and-egg phenomenon. Seeing and owning our phoniness gives us the awareness and sometimes the motivation to move along the continuum toward authenticity, which can allow our team to have more psychological safety.

Honest

In the middle of the Authenticity Continuum we have honesty. "Honesty is the best policy," right? But have you ever been honest about something and it backfired? At one time or another, all of us have upset someone, spoken out of turn, offended others, or said something we regretted. You may also notice that not everyone likes your honesty, agrees with your honesty, or seems all that interested in hearing what you honestly have to say, for a variety of reasons.

Honesty seems straightforward, universally encouraged, and positive, but it's more complicated than that. We all have had experiences in life and at work when being honest created more trust and connection in a particular relationship, as well as more psychological safety within a group. However, we've also had the painful experience of honesty having the opposite effect—causing less trust, connection, and safety.

Based on this, over the course of our lives, and particularly in our careers, most of us learn how to tactfully "massage" the truth. We end up saying to ourselves, *I don't want to be phony. I want to be honest—but "mostly" honest, in a way that makes me look good, doesn't get me into trouble, and has the people I work with respect, admire, and trust me.*

We end up spending a lot of time and energy on this side of the Authenticity Continuum, trying to figure out how honest we can be with certain people and in specific situations. This is how most of us are trained to operate at work . . . and it's exhausting. Often our level of honesty has a lot to do with how much psychological safety exists in the environment. The safer we feel, the easier it is for us to be honest. And the more honesty we have within the team, usually the more psychologically safe we feel.

However, if we just stop at honesty but don't get all the way to authenticity, there are ways that honesty can actually stifle psychological safety, because when people are worried about being "called out" in a brutally honest way, they may be afraid to speak up or make mistakes.

Where there's real freedom and power for us and our team is on the other side of honesty. Yes, we must be honest, which takes courage in and of itself; but for us to get to authenticity (which is foundational to psychological safety), we have to remove something from our honesty and add something to it. The thing we have to remove is our *self-righteousness*. And what we have to add is *vulnerability*.

Removing Self-Righteousness

Self-righteousness can sometimes be hard for us to fully understand and own up to. Many of us are quite opinionated, and will happily share our opinions openly. The issue isn't with our opinions or even our willingness to express them passionately; it's the self-righteousness with which we hold our opinions that can be problematic. When we hold an opinion with self-righteousness, whether or not we express it, we are coming from a place of *being right*. And if I'm *right* about something and you don't agree with me, what does that make you?

Wrong.

Now we have a problem.

Self-righteousness separates us from others. In certain relationships, situations, and environments, we might be open and honest enough with other people to let them know directly that we think they're wrong. We might be able to say straight to their face something like, "I think that's a bad idea!" But more often than not and especially

18

at work, we bite our tongue in such situations, especially if there is a lack of trust in our relationship with the person or a lack of psychological safety within the group. We may say, "Thanks for your input; I'll take that into consideration." And then we might leave the room, find someone we agree with, and say, "There's no way we're doing that!" And then, we'll continue to find others who agree with us and we'll gather evidence for why we're right and those who don't see it "our way" are wrong.

Self-righteousness negatively impacts us, our relationships, and our teams. It also undercuts our ability to influence those around us and fundamentally damages individual trust in our relationships and the psychological safety of our teams.

Identifying self-righteousness can be challenging because often when you and I are being self-righteous, we don't think we're being self-righteous, we just think we're *right*. It takes quite a bit of self-awareness to notice our self-righteousness, and it takes willingness and maturity to let it go, or to at least look at things from a different perspective. It can also be helpful to have people around us whom we trust to point out when we're being self-righteous but may not be aware of it.

I'm grateful, most of the time, that I have people in my life—friends, family members, and people on my team— who are willing to point out my self-righteousness to me.

A few years ago, I was in the car with my wife, Michelle, and our daughters, Samantha and Rosie. We were backing out of the garage at our house. We were in the car that Michelle normally drives, but I was driving. Our two cars are parked pretty close to one another in our garage, so when you back out, you have to be careful not to hit the other car on one side of you and not to get the side mirror clipped on the other side.

As I was backing out that day, I noticed that the car seemed to be parked at a bit of an angle, and I was having a hard time. Although I do drive her car from time to time, I'm used to being in the other car and on the other side of the garage. As I continued to back out and struggle, I stopped and turned to Michelle.

"Babe, you know, if you park your car just like this," I said, motioning with my hands, pointing out some visual cues in the garage, "it makes it much easier to back it out."

As I was saying this, Rosie, who was sitting right behind me in the car, said, "Hey Dad, stop 'mansplaining' to Mom."

When she said this, I was taken aback at first. She was nine years old at the time, and I was actually quite impressed that she knew what "mansplaining" meant, (when men arrogantly and condescendingly explain things, usually to women, that they already know . . . kind of like how I'm explaining this to you right now, especially if you're already familiar with this term). Even though I was proud of Rosie for knowing this, I immediately defended myself, saying, "I was not mansplaining to Mom."

Then I looked at Michelle sitting next to me, and then at Samantha and Rosie in the back seat, and they all said in unison, "Yes you were!"

Their feedback stopped me in my tracks. I paused, checked in with myself, and listened to what they were saying. Then I said to Michelle with a sheepish laugh, "Sorry, babe."

What had just happened? I was feeling uncomfortable with the backing-out situation; it wasn't working for me or set up exactly the way I would've liked it. Instead of acknowledging my own discomfort, I decided that was the precise moment for me to coach Michelle on the "proper" way to park the car in the garage. I bet you're not surprised that she didn't respond by saying, "Thank you for pointing that out—do you have any more feedback for me?" No, of course she didn't. Why? Because I was being self-righteous. I hadn't asked if she wanted my feedback. And, even though I said it in a "nice" and "helpful" way, the underlying message I was communicating to her in that moment was that I park the car the "right" way, and she parks the car the "wrong" way. In other words, "I'm superior, you're inferior." I imagine you can relate to one or both sides of this dynamic personally?

The Difference Between Self-Righteousness and Conviction

Removing self-righteousness does not mean watering down our opinions, decreasing our passion, or withholding our feedback. Believing strongly in our opinions, as well as in our values and beliefs about life, work, and everything else, is important. However, understanding the difference between conviction and self-righteousness is essential. When we're coming from a place of conviction about something, we believe it to be true and we're willing to speak up about it, to defend our position, or to engage in healthy dialogue or debate about it. These are all important aspects of building strong and trusting relationships with those around us, and with having healthy discussions and debates within our team. Being able to do this is one of the most important benefits of having psychological safety. As Amy Edmondson told me, "Psychological safety is not about being 'nice' or even about creating 'safe spaces' where everyone feels comfortable all the time. It's about having enough trust, respect, and courage to engage with each other in a way that allows everyone to do their best work."

Conviction, however, is also about having the humility, awareness, and maturity to consider we might be wrong—or that, at the very least, there may be other ways to look at whatever it is we're discussing or debating, even if we don't see it that way ourselves.

When we cross over into self-righteousness, we're no longer interested in hearing what anyone else has to say if they disagree with us or have a different perspective. We're *right* and anyone and everyone who doesn't see it our way is *wrong*. This often shuts down the discussion and can create an intense "Us vs. Them" dynamic that negatively impacts everyone involved, the team, and won't allow for real authenticity or psychological safety.

Self-righteousness separates us from those who don't think like we do or hold the same ideas, opinions, or beliefs. At work this leads to disconnection, unresolved conflicts, and factions within teams and organizations. Lines get drawn between departments, offices, regions, and levels within the company, making it more difficult to make decisions, collaborate, and get things done in a psychologically safe and effective way.

The natural human response to self-righteousness is defensiveness, which is why when we're being self-righteous it's almost impossible to influence others. If we want to connect with those around us in a real way, and create an environment of authenticity, trust, collaboration, and, most specifically, psychological safety, we must be willing to recognize, own, and remove our self-righteousness. Conviction is healthy and important. Self-righteousness is damaging and destructive.

Adding Vulnerability

Vulnerability is fundamental to relationships, trust, authenticity, and, of course, psychological safety. However, it's often misunderstood. Most of us have a strange relationship to vulnerability. Dr. Brené Brown is a well-known research professor at the University of Houston and best-selling author who studies human emotions, including vulnerability. Her research has had a big impact on both my work and my personal life. She defines vulnerability as "uncertainty, risk, and emotional exposure." I love this succinct definition. Can you think of anything meaningful or important that you've ever accomplished or experienced in your life (personally or professional), that did not involve uncertainty, risk, or emotional exposure? If something matters to us (a job, a project, a relationship, a goal, the team, or anything else), it's going to require one, two, or all three of these things.

Even though vulnerability can be scary and uncomfortable, when we're willing to lean into it, it's incredibly beneficial to us, those around us, and our teams for a few important reasons.

First, it's fundamental to human trust and connection. So, if we're going to have real psychological safety on our team, it's essential that we trust one another, connect with each other, and create a culture that is conducive to these essential things. Second, vulnerability is necessary for creativity, innovation, change, risk, and anything new or different. Since the essence of psychological safety is about creating an environment on the team that allows people to speak up, try new things, and not worry about being shamed, ridiculed, or kicked out of the group for doing so, it's paramount that the leader and team members be willing to operate vulnerably with one another.

Being vulnerable takes courage. Unfortunately, all too often we relate to vulnerability—especially in certain environments, relationships, and situations (particularly at work and with our team)—as something we should avoid. But it's vulnerability that liberates us from our erroneous and insatiable obsession with trying to do everything "right"—thinking that we can't make mistakes, have flaws, or be human. Embracing vulnerability allows us to let go of the pressure-filled demands for perfection that we place on ourselves.

In addition to liberating us, being vulnerable gives other people permission to be vulnerable as well; and in doing so, we open up the possibility of real human connection and courage.

As Brené Brown says, "There is no courage without vulnerability. When we build cultures at work where there is zero tolerance for vulnerability, no open conversations happen. We end up talking *about* each other instead of *to* each other."

The natural human response to vulnerability is empathy. And with empathy, we can create deeper trust and understanding with those around us. These things are essential for psychological safety to exist on our team.

The Authenticity Equation

Moving along the Authenticity Continuum—from phony, to honest, and then to authentic—a key concept of my work and my research on authenticity has led me to think of it as an equation:

Honesty – Self-Righteousness + Vulnerability = Authenticity

When we notice our own phony tendencies, challenge ourselves to be honest, remove our self-righteousness, and find the courage to be vulnerable we're able to be truly *authentic.*

Understanding the Authenticity Equation and practicing it with ourselves, our team, and everyone allows us to show up and connect with others in a real way. It's not easy, and it takes significant self-awareness and courage, but when we do this, it's both liberating for us and inspiring for those around us. At the core, psychological safety is based on our ability and the ability of those on our team to be authentic in this way.

Lower the Waterline on Your Iceberg

The metaphor I've used for many years when talking about authenticity is the iceberg. While this is a simple and often-used metaphor, it fits perfectly. Most of us feel comfortable showing just the tip of our iceberg—the professional, appropriate, and put-together aspects of ourselves. But who we really are, what we really think, how we really feel, and what's really going on for us is below the waterline. By lowering the waterline, we can show up more authentically and create more psychological safety around us.

There's an exercise I use to encourage teams to lower their waterline. It's called "If you really knew me . . . ." I learned this exercise a long time ago from my friends and mentors Rich and Yvonne Dutra-St. John. They are the co-founders of a wonderful nonprofit organization called Challenge Day. This powerful exercise gives people the opportunity to be real and vulnerable with others, and allows groups and teams to connect with each other in an authentic way—thus creating more psychological safety.

I've led this exercise hundreds of times over the past decade or so. I do it in big groups, small groups, and with intact teams of people who work together on a daily basis, which is one of my favorite ways to do the exercise.

I've written specifically about this exercise in three of my four previous books because I've seen this process have such a profound impact on the people, leaders, and teams I work with. It's one of the best ways I know to create trust and connection in the moment. And, the more willing and often a team is able to lower their waterline with each other, the more likely they are to deepen the psychological safety within their group.

I was invited to deliver a team development program for the marketing leadership team at Pandora at an offsite they were having in Carmel, California, a few years ago. Pandora's chief marketing officer at the time, Aimée Lapic, had been in her role for a year and a half. Her team had grown and changed during this time, and the company was going through quite a bit of change also. Overall, things were going pretty well, but this offsite was an opportunity for the eight-person leadership team to connect, reflect, and plan. And, since half of the team worked out of the company headquarters in Oakland, and the other half of the team was located in the New York City office, it was a good opportunity to spend some quality time with one another discussing some of the most important issues, goals, and challenges they were facing.

The program I delivered for them came at the end of a multiday offsite, which had seemed to go well. We discussed the Authenticity Continuum and the

Authenticity Equation, as well as the importance of psychological safety and lowering the waterline.

When the time was right, I said, "We're going to do an exercise now that will allow us to be vulnerable with one another and connect more deeply. In a moment we'll go around the table, and everyone will have a few minutes to talk," I explained. "I'll go first. When it's your turn, you're just going to repeat this phrase, 'If you really knew me, you'd know this about me . . . ' and then you can lower the waterline on your iceberg. There's no right or wrong way to do the exercise, and you don't have to say anything you don't want to say. However, I invite you and challenge you to really go there and allow yourself to be vulnerable with your team." I went on to say, "To make it as safe as possible, I'm going to ask that we not say anything to the person who is talking—no advice, questions, or comments—just listening. And, additionally, let's all agree to keep whatever is said here confidential. Can we all agree to this?"

Everyone nodded in agreement and then I started, "If you really knew me, you'd know that I'm feeling excited and grateful to be here with you all, and nervous to be having this risky conversation with you. If you really, really knew me, you'd know that I love the work that I do, and sometimes I notice it's much easier for me to talk about being authentic, engaging in healthy conflict, and taking risks than it is to actually do these things in my work and my life. And, if you really, really, really knew me, you'd know that although it has been a few years and I've done a lot of grief work, I still find myself feeling disoriented and sad because of the deaths of both of my parents and especially my sister Lori, who died just a few years ago. It feels weird and lonely to be the only living member of my nuclear family, especially at my age."

I finished sharing and then turned to Aimée, who happened to be sitting to my left. "Now it's your turn," I said to her.

She took a deep breath and lowered the waterline on her iceberg. Aimée shared in an authentic and courageous way about how she was feeling, and specifically some of her fears as well as her hopes as they related to the team and the company. She then shared some of what was going on in her life personally in a vulnerable way. What she said and how she said it was powerful and courageous, and it gave everyone else on the team permission to go there themselves, which they did.

We went around the entire table and each member of the team lowered the waterline on their iceberg and shared vulnerably how they were feeling and what was going on for them in that moment. There were some tears, some laughs, and some pats on the back. It was a poignant and bonding moment for the team.

Deep down below the waterline we get to some pretty basic and important human experiences and emotions—fear, joy, sadness, gratitude, anger, hope, hurt, uncertainty, risk, and, ultimately, vulnerability. And when we get in touch with these emotions and feel safe enough to express them to the people around us, it's both liberating and connecting. Once we were finished, the bonding nature of this courageous conversation was palpable among the team members. And the follow-up discussion, as often is the case, allowed the team to not only connect more deeply, but to talk about ways to stay connected and support one another in their work, as leaders, as a team, and as human beings.

The work that Pandora's marketing leadership team did in this exercise paid off. They came out of that retreat more connected to one another and with a deeper level of trust and psychological safety. Aimée told me that it was a game-changer for them. Over the course of the next few months the company went through even more changes as it was purchased by SiriusXM. And although this big change had a major impact on the organization and on the marketing team specifically, Aimée's ability to operate with authenticity as a leader and the fact that she and her team had created such a strong sense of psychological safety allowed them to navigate the changes and challenges they faced much more effectively and to lean on each other in the process.

I've done this exercise with groups of all kinds—in different industries, cities, and countries, and facing all kinds of circumstances. What I'm constantly reminded of when we have this conversation is that down below the waterline we're all so similar. One of the great paradoxes of life, business, and teamwork is that while we're diverse in many important ways, we also have so much common ground as fellow human beings. As simple of a realization as this is, it's important for us to remind ourselves and each other to create opportunities as often as we can to experience genuine human connection. Authenticity is an in-the-moment phenomenon, and lowering our waterline and encouraging others to do the same is how we build more authentic relationships, enhance trust, and expand the psychological safety of our team.

🧩 If You Really Knew Me . . . 🧩

This exercise can be incredibly powerful in terms of building more trust and psychological safety. For it to be done safely and effectively, please follow these instructions carefully.

You can facilitate this exercise with your team or any other group, as well as in a one-on-one meeting. If you do it in a group, it's best for there to be 15 people or fewer. For larger groups, it's ideal to break up into smaller segments, given the intimate nature of this process.

To set up the exercise, lead off with a general overview of the importance of authenticity and the iceberg metaphor. Then, talk about the Authenticity Continuum and the Authenticity Equation concepts. In addition to explaining these things verbally, feel free to write them out on a dry erase board or flip chart. This exercise is all about creating connection, trust, empathy, and psychological safety for everyone involved.

Once you have shared some key information about authenticity and the context for the exercise, it's important to create a safe environment. Here are three ground rules to help achieve this:

1. You don't have to say anything you don't want to say.

2. No one will be specifically commenting on what is shared, or giving unsolicited feedback.

3. Whatever is said will be kept strictly confidential and will not leave the room.

After the ground rules are established and everyone agrees, the most important aspect of facilitating this exercise is a genuine willingness to be vulnerable, and go deep. The more open and vulnerable you are, the more permission you give to the group. Don't play it safe or try to say the *right* thing; just be real and really lower your waterline. You go first by saying the following:

If you knew me, you'd know that . . .

If you really, really knew me, you'd know that . . .

And, if you really, really, really knew me, you'd know that . . .

When you're finished, let the person to your left speak, and repeat until every group member has shared individually, repeated these statements themselves, and lowered their waterline.

Be sure to have a follow-up discussion to give the team an opportunity to reflect on the experience: how it was for them personally, what they noticed listening to others share, and if they have anything else they want to add. A great question to ask the group is, "How many of you could relate to what people were saying?" Most people will acknowledge that they could, in fact, relate to what others shared. The reason we can relate when people lower the waterline is that the natural human response to vulnerability is empathy. And, because down below the waterline we're way more alike than we are different.

Finish the exercise by thanking everyone for their courage to participate, and by talking about practical ways you and everyone involved can operate with more authenticity.

The Leader's Role in Creating Psychological Safety

Leaders, like Aimée at Pandora, have a significant role in creating psychological safety for their teams. How leaders show up, communicate, and operate, and what they focus on has a big impact on the team and the culture.

According to Amy Edmondson's research at Harvard, there are three things that leaders can do to help create, enhance, and maintain psychological safety:

Frame work as learning problems, as opposed to execution problems. Edmondson says, "Make explicit that there is enormous uncertainty ahead and enormous interdependence. In other words, be clear that there are areas that still require explanation, and so each team member's input matters. For example, saying things like 'We've never been here before, we can't know what will happen, so we've got to have everybody's brains and voices in the game,' helps create this atmosphere."

Acknowledge your own fallibility. "Make simple statements that encourage peers and subordinates to speak up, such as, 'I may miss something—I need to hear from you,'" Edmondson says.

Model curiosity by asking a lot of questions. According to Edmondson, asking a lot of questions "actually creates a necessity for voice, because team members will feel a need to respond." The more a leader focuses on curiosity and learning, the easier it becomes for people on the team to speak up, ask questions, and embrace the discomfort of not knowing, all of which are essential for growth and psychological safety.

When we, as leaders, are willing to operate with authenticity, we can build more personal credibility with our teams, which then leads to greater psychological safety. And it's important to remember that there are two types of credibility: professional and personal. Professional credibility is about our résumé, our track record, our title, where we went to school, the results we've produced in the past, our skills, and other tangible things. Professional credibility is clearly important. In many cases, however—especially for the purpose of building trust, a strong team culture, and real psychological safety—personal credibility is much more important. Personal credibility has to do with people being able to relate to us, trust us, understand us, and find common ground with us—and with our ability to do these things with them in return. We build personal credibility with others by listening to them, opening up to them, sharing about ourselves, caring about them, apologizing when necessary, and being willing to lower the waterline on our iceberg. As we've discussed, self-righteousness damages our personal credibility and vulnerability enhances it. The best way for us to build personal credibility with others is to be authentic.

When we have personal credibility, there is more connection, loyalty, and understanding. We can give and receive feedback, work through challenges, and navigate ups and downs together. We see each other as real people, not just as titles or résumés. And, ultimately enhancing our personal credibility is one of the key things we can do as leaders to increase the psychological safety of the team.

The Team Member's Role in Creating Psychological Safety

While leaders definitely have a responsibility to do everything they can to foster psychological safety, great teams understand that it's more than just the leader who provides this type of environment—it's up to the entire team. As team members, there are a few important things to think about, understand, and do if we want our team to be as psychologically safe as possible:

Ask for help. Most of us enjoy helping others but aren't so great asking for help ourselves. It takes courage, requires vulnerability, and exemplifies trust when we ask for help from those around us. Even though it can be scary, when we do it we're able to get some much-needed support, we empower others (because people like to help), and we make it safer for everyone on the team to ask for help when they need it.

Take ownership. The culture of any team is made up of the attitudes, mindsets, and behaviors of everyone on the team. Sure, the leader of the team has a significant impact on the culture and how safe (or unsafe) the team is. However, when we as individual team members take ownership, we're less likely to complain and gossip and more likely to contribute to the overall success of the team. From an ownership perspective, it's important for us to be mindful of what we're doing and saying to make sure we're contributing to the psychological safety of the group. And if there is something anyone else is doing or saying that is negatively impacting the psychological safety of our team, we can address it directly in order to make things better for us and everyone else.

Lead by example. The things that are important for leaders to exhibit in creating the kind of psychological safety we just discussed—framing work as learning problems, acknowledging your own fallibility, and being curious/asking questions—are not only essential behaviors for leaders, they're also essential for everyone on the team. When individual team members take this approach and lead by example, it makes the leader's job easier and increases the psychological safety of the group exponentially.

How Psychologically Safe Is Your Team?

If you want your team to have more psychological safety, it's important to think about it, talk about it, and look at ways to enhance it with those you work with directly. To measure your team's level of psychological safety, ask yourself and those on your team how strongly you and they agree or disagree with these statements:

1. If you make a mistake on this team, it's often held against you.

2. Members of this team are able to bring up problems and tough issues.

3. People on this team sometimes reject others for being different.

4. It's safe to take a risk on this team.

5. It's difficult to ask other members of this team for help.

6. No one on this team would deliberately act in a way that undermines my efforts.

7. Working with members of this team,
    my unique skills and talents are valued
    and utilized.

How strongly you and those on your team agree (or disagree) with these statements speaks directly to the level of psychological safety that exists within your group. This can be a great discussion for you and your team to have at an offsite, retreat, or meeting.

What the Entire Team Can Do to Create More Psychological Safety

Regardless of how strong the psychological safety is on your team, there are specific things the team as a whole can do together to enhance it. In addition to the various ideas we've discussed throughout this chapter, here are some things you can do as a group to create more psychological safety:

Take time to think about, talk about, and explore psychological safety. It's important to carve out time to think about, talk about, and discuss the culture of the team in general, and your psychological safety specifically. The questions in the previous section are ones you can use to help start the discussion as you assess how psychologically safe (or not) your team may currently be. Having a regular cadence of meetings and offsites, with specific time dedicated to focusing on the health of the team, the culture, and discussing anything that's either getting in the way of psychological safety or can enhance it, is *essential* to the success of your team.

Doing this, of course, can be really challenging if there isn't much psychological safety on your team right now. If that is the case, it's best to start with some baby steps—talking to the leader of your team or one key member initially, and building from there. Even if your team has a good amount of psychological safety or the issues you may have with any aspect of your team culture seem fairly "normal," it takes real commitment and courage to address these things and make time to discuss them consistently.

Talk about mistakes. The research clearly shows that teams with higher psychological safety are much more willing to admit and talk about their mistakes. This allows everyone to learn and grow, and makes it much less taboo and scary both to make mistakes and to address them openly. Ironically, the more willing we are to talk about our mistakes, the less likely we are to make them. This freedom allows us to do our best, most innovative work.

Check in with each other regularly. It's important for teams to check in with each other one-on-one and as a group on a consistent basis. Having a regular cadence of one-on-one meetings, team meetings, and offsites is important. And, when those meetings take place, making sure there is a little bit of time for people to actually check in with each other personally is important. If you have time to do the "If you really knew me . . . " exercise together, that's ideal. But even just a moment or two of a check-in—asking people how they're doing, and *really listening*—can make a big difference in terms of building and maintaining personal connections. Remember: We're all human beings, with full and complex lives, doing the best we can.

Encourage risk-taking. Challenge yourself and each other to take risks, step out of your comfort zone, and try new things. The more we do this, along with being willing to acknowledge and talk about mistakes, the more freedom everyone on the team will have to experiment and truly go for it. Teams that encourage healthy risk-taking are much more likely to succeed and create more psychological safety when they remember that "playing it safe" isn't the goal.

Have fun together. One of the easiest and most enjoyable ways to build more trust, connection, and psychological safety on your team is to create time to just hang out and have fun together. Over the years of working with lots of teams, I've seen the incredible value of spending time together, getting to know each other on a personal and human level, and just having a good time with one another. This is not only enjoyable, it's bonding and can go such a long way toward building connection, culture, and safety for your team.

Psychological safety is about creating a team environment that is conducive to trust, risk-taking, growth, collaboration, and performance. It's the foundation of teamwork and is fundamental to our success. And, although it can be challenging, there are a number of things we can do as leaders, as team members, and as teams to create, enhance, deepen, and maintain the psychological safety of our group, thus putting us in the best position to thrive.

FOCUS ON INCLUSION
AND BELONGING

I made the varsity basketball team my junior year at Skyline High School in Oakland, one of the most ethnically diverse cities in the United States. Making the team was a big deal for a few reasons. First of all, I wasn't nearly as good at basketball as I was at baseball. Second, our basketball program was *really* competitive; we'd come very close to winning the state championship each of the previous two seasons, and two Skyline alumni, Gary Payton and Greg Foster, were playing in the NBA at that time.

I was really excited that I made it, but also nervous. I wasn't sure how much I would get to play, and I was a bit intimidated by the talent on our team and in our league. In addition, I was the only white kid. The rest of my teammates were African American. And, as I would come to find out as the season progressed, I was the only white player on any of the six public high school basketball teams in Oakland that year—making me the only white kid *in our entire league.* I knew all the guys and felt pretty comfortable on the team, but when we would walk into other school's gyms, I often became acutely aware of the difference between me and my teammates.

One night we were playing a nonleague game against Amador Valley High School, in Pleasanton, California. This school was only about 25 miles from Skyline, but it was very different. All the kids on the basketball team, and most of the students and fans in the gym that night, were white. As we were warming up, I could hear some murmurs and laughs in the crowd pointed in my direction. I tried not to pay too much attention to them, and to just focus on getting ready to play.

I came off the bench and into the game late in the first quarter, and the crowd started jeering and heckling me a bit. A few minutes later, I got fouled as I drove to the basket for a layup. I went to the free throw line for my two shots. As I got to the line and the ref gave me the ball, the crowd began to chant, "Whiiiiite boy, whiiiiite boy," as they stood, waved their hands back and forth, and laughed at me.

It's fairly common for the people in the stands at basketball games to taunt the visiting team, especially when a player goes to the free throw line, because it's usually quiet and they're trying to disrupt the player's focus. Although I'd been taunted many times in my life playing sports and otherwise, and had definitely been called "white boy" a lot, there was something about this moment that was really upsetting to me. Looking up into that crowd, seeing all of those faces that looked similar to mine, and hearing them make fun of me because I was the only white kid on the team was both confusing and painful. I tried to laugh it off and not let it get to me, but I felt really alone in that moment and like I didn't belong— on my own team, on the court, and in that gym.

Although it was hard for me to fully understand at the time, I learned a lot from the experience that night and from being on that team. Some of the lessons were difficult and scary, but most of them were enlightening, especially as I reflect back on them now. It gave me a sustained visceral and emotional experience of what it's like to be different from those around me.

I spent a good part of my adolescent years in the minority racially on most of my teams and in school. My high school graduating class of around 500 students was less than 20 percent white, and was about 40 percent African American and 30 percent Asian American. The music we listened to, clothes we wore, movies we saw, TV shows we watched, and much else was influenced by those around me and the strong African American culture of my high school, city, and social group.

My cultural development continued in a new way when I got to Stanford. I immediately noticed many differences. There were kids from all over the United States and even a few from other countries. And while there was definitely some diversity, it was much more limited compared to where I grew up, which, ironically, was less than an hour's drive from campus. When my friends from Oakland would ask me, "What's it like at Stanford?" My response in those first few months was often, "It's cool, but really different here. I've never been around this many white people in my life."

Given some of these dynamics, my own confusion about who I was and where I fit in, and my interest in understanding racial and cultural differences from both a sociological and historical perspective, I decided to major in American studies, with a specialization in race and ethnicity. And over the course of my time at Stanford, I was exposed to even more people with different backgrounds and perspectives than mine, although on the surface many of us looked the same.

Lots of the guys on my baseball team came from wealthy families and much more conservative parts of the state and country than I did. Once I moved past my fear and judgment, I found them and their families to be incredibly kind, welcoming, and supportive.

Then I got drafted by the Kansas City Royals and signed my pro contract. I assumed things would be very different culturally in the minor leagues than they were at Stanford and in Oakland, and I was right. In addition to my teammates having different backgrounds in terms of their levels of education, where they came from in the country, as well as their race and ethnicity, there were also a number of players from outside the U.S.—specifically from the Dominican Republic, Puerto Rico, Venezuela, and Mexico.

While there was some racial, educational, and ideological tension that existed, I learned a great deal from my teammates and appreciated the ways in which we could find common ground—both in our mutual love for baseball, and as young men pursuing our dreams and trying to make our way in the world.

After my baseball career ended abruptly, I found myself back living in Oakland and working in San Francisco for an Internet company. I was now 25 years old and meeting people from all walks of life both at work and outside of work. I found myself in a whole new realm—no longer in school or in sports, but out in the "real" world, interacting with people of all ages, races, orientations, and more. My team experience now focused on work, not sports, and my teammates were both men and women, with different skills, backgrounds, and perspectives. It was exciting and confusing at the same time, for many reasons. I learned a lot in a fairly short period of time and could see that although my experiences in sports were very different from what I was encountering in business, there were many similarities in what it takes for diverse groups of people to come together and create a successful team.

When I began the process of starting my own business as a coach, speaker, and writer, my initial thought was to focus on diversity, due to the importance of the topic, and also because of my background, interest, and education. However, I remember thinking at the time, *Who wants to hear a young, white, straight man talk about diversity? No one will listen to me or take me seriously, and it's possible I'll upset and offend a lot of people in the process.*

I did start my business in 2001, and decided initially to focus on personal development, communication, and teamwork as my primary topics. Even as my work has expanded over the years and issues of diversity, inclusion, and belonging have continued to be important to me (not to mention fundamental to the leaders, teams, and organizations I work with), I've been hesitant to engage in these topics directly. It seemed to me that these issues were best and most appropriately addressed by people from specific communities who are directly impacted and have more lived experience in this regard than I do. There are so many incredible thought leaders in the diversity and inclusion space who have researched, written about, and boldly been the leading voices on these important topics. And the vast majority of these leaders are people of color, women, members of the LGBTQ community, and those who self-identify as members of one or more minority groups.

I didn't believe my voice, perspective, or insight were wanted, needed, or even credible. For a number of reasons,

I now realize this is not true. My avoidance in addressing these things directly is both an example of my own privilege and a fear-based justification to protect myself from potential discomfort, ridicule, and disconnection.

I believe that now more than ever it's time for all of us to be willing to engage in these conversations and address these important, yet often challenging, painful, and uncomfortable issues. If our teams are going to thrive, and we're going to create a culture of trust and high performance, we have to be willing to think about, talk about, and engage in discussions about diversity and inclusion, and we have to take consistent actions to create, maintain, and expand an environment where everyone on the team and in our organization feels a true sense of belonging.

As we dive more deeply into this chapter and this topic, I want to clarify and define briefly what I mean when I use the words *diversity, inclusion,* and *belonging* in the context of our discussion in this book.

Diversity refers to teams and organizations that are composed of employees with varying characteristics including, but not limited to, race, religious and political beliefs, gender, sexual orientation, ethnicity, education, socioeconomic background, gender identity, geographic location, physical ability, and age. Representation like this is important, and as Google CEO Sundar Pichai says, "A diverse mix of voices leads to better discussions, decisions, and outcomes for everyone."

Inclusion is about having respect for and appreciation of the various differences of everyone on the team and in the organization. It also means actively involving everyone's ideas, knowledge, perspectives, approaches, and styles to maximize the success of the team and doing everything possible to not consciously or unconsciously exclude people. Verna Myers, vice president of inclusion strategy at Netflix, clarifies it this way: "Diversity is being invited to the party. Inclusion is being asked to dance."

Belonging is a fundamental and universal human need. It's about creating an environment on our team and in our organization where everyone, regardless of their diverse characteristics and background, feels safe to be themselves and knows that they're an integral part of the group. According to Pat Wadors, chief talent officer at ServiceNow, "While policies of inclusion can ensure that everyone is invited, it's a sense of belonging that allows workers to feel safe, valued, and seen."

In this chapter and book, we're focusing heavily on inclusion and belonging. But diversity is also incredibly important, so let's take a few moments to talk about it briefly. If you're an owner, an executive, or a leader who has specific influence over who gets hired and promoted on your team or in your organization, focusing on diversity is essential.

An overwhelming amount of research in recent years has proved that diverse teams and organizations perform better than those that aren't. According to a report called "Delivering through Diversity" published by McKinsey & Co. in 2018 that I mentioned in the Introduction, ethnically diverse companies outperform their peers by 33 percent, and gender-diverse companies outperform their peers by 21 percent. Additionally, having your team and your company be as reflective as possible of the culture and, specifically, your customer base, is an important advantage in today's global economy. Seventy-nine percent of respondents to Deloitte's 2017 Global Human Capital Trends survey said diversity is a competitive advantage, with 39 percent noting that it's a "significant" competitive advantage. Clearly, expanding the diversity of your team and company has a lot to do with filling the talent pipeline with as diverse a group of people as possible.

Eric Severson is currently an executive vice president and the chief people officer at Neiman Marcus. When I spoke with him on my podcast in early 2019, he was DaVita's chief people officer at that time. Eric is a passionate advocate for diversity, inclusion, and belonging. During our interview, he said, "We will always hire the most qualified person for the job, period. All of our efforts around diversity are about filling the pool of candidates from whom to select with qualified people from all walks of life, and then allowing everyone to compete equally for the role."

There are so many evidenced-based hiring approaches these days that can assist companies in expanding the diversity of their teams, leadership, and overall organization. We still clearly have a lot of work to do in this regard. And, focusing on diversity is essential for the success of your team and organization.

As important as diversity is from a culture, engagement, and performance standpoint, one of the best things that team members, leaders, and teams as a whole can do is to focus on inclusion and belonging. And, as essential as these things are to the success of your team, they can also be complicated and challenging. Here are some of the things that make it difficult both to discuss these important topics and to create environments of real inclusion and belonging.

It can be scary. Talking about issues of race, gender, orientation, age, diversity, and inclusion can be intimi -dating. For those of us, like myself, who are members of majority groups in our work environment (in my case, being white, male, straight, cisgender, affluent, a native English speaker, nondisabled, etc.), there is often quite a bit of fear of being judged, attacked, hurting or offending others, or being perceived as racist, sexist, homophobic, or in any way prejudiced. Despite my experiences growing up, I obviously have no idea what it's like to be a person of color, female, gay, disabled, transgender, or to be a member of any other minority group. Even with my interest and education with respect to these topics, it's still quite vulnerable and uncomfortable for me to address them directly, especially in certain environments, with specific people, and in certain contexts. Writing about these things here in this book, while fundamental to the overall topic of team culture and performance, and to the work that I do more broadly, is scary. Even as I write these words, I can feel myself worrying about what you will think about my thoughts, ideas, and perspectives on these important and sensitive issues.

Robin DiAngelo, an expert in multicultural education and a professor at the University of Washington, asserts in her best-selling book, *White Fragility: Why It's so Hard for White People to Talk about Racism*, that for many white people, the mere mention or accusation of racism is often seen as even more offensive than the fact or practice of it. In other words, there are those who are more concerned about being called racist than they are about paying attention to the detrimental impact racism actually has.

For women, people of color, members of the LGBTQ community, and other people who self-identify as belonging to various minority communities that I've talked to about these things over the years, understandably there can be a lot of fear and frustration—not wanting to always be the one who has to bring these issues up, experiencing intense backlash and repercussions for doing so, or simply not feeling safe enough.

In today's political and cultural environment, things have gotten so divisive and intense about many issues, but none more than these. This divisiveness and intensity have made it even harder and scarier to address these topics in an honest and productive way. I was listening to an episode of Marc Maron's *WTF* podcast in which he was interviewing Brené Brown. Marc said, "If we're going to generalize where we're at these days, I think the political right's way of dealing seems to be 'never apologize,' and double down if necessary. And, on the political left, it's 'never forgive.'" While this may be a bit of an overgeneralization or simplification of where things are, I believe, sadly, there's real truth in what he said, which adds to the challenge of how we engage in these important discussions and dynamics.

Regardless of our specific race, gender, political affiliation, or background—for a number of reasons and due to the personal, emotional, and complex nature of these issues—it can be incredibly uncomfortable for us to address these things directly and effectively.

We don't see things the same way. Our perspectives and opinions vary quite a bit about many things. In regard to the sensitive topics of inclusion and belonging, the difference in how we see things, as well as how we experience life, comes into play in a significant way. Even if we do our best to pay attention to others and listen to their perspective, and if we try to have empathy and compassion for other people's experiences, it's still hard to walk in someone else's shoes. We all have blind spots.

I'm constantly humbled by this. A few years ago, Michelle and I attended a relationship workshop in San Francisco. There were roughly 70 people in the room, about half men and half women.

At one point during the program, the woman leading the workshop asked us men when was the last time we could remember feeling physically unsafe. She said, "I'm going to name off some specific time frames, and I would like you to raise your hand, just once, for the time frame that is appropriate for you. Was it in the last 10 years? Five years? One year? Six months? Three months? One month? One week? Or 24 hours?"

She paused for a moment as she said each time frame, so that we could answer accordingly. I raised my hand when she said one year, remembering back to a time months before when I had felt specifically scared about my own physical safety. It was late one night on a business trip when I was walking back to my hotel room alone in Washington, D.C. I got a bit lost, and there were very few people out, which made me feel scared and concerned for my safety. Some of the other men in the room had also raised their hands at the same time I did, although some raised them shortly before and after me.

She then asked the women the same question, and as she was going through the same list of time frames, the women weren't raising their hands, which seemed a bit odd to me. When she got to within the last week, a few hands went up. Then she asked, "Within the last 24 hours?" At this point, just about every woman's hand in the room went up, including Michelle's. She was sitting right next to me, and I turned to her a bit startled, with a shocked look on my face, thinking to myself, *When? Where? Why?* With my mouth wide open, I started to look around the room at all the hands in the air. Many of the women had looks on their faces as if to say, *How did you guys not know this was our experience?* And most of the men in the room, including me, were looking around in astonishment wondering, *How is this possible?*

The workshop leader then said, "This is one of the many fundamental differences between the experience of walking around in a female body versus walking around in a male body. And we almost never even talk about it or address it directly."

Even if we pay attention, listen, learn, and try to understand what other people's experiences are, it can still be hard to fully relate. I was raised by a feminist single mom who talked about gender inequality a lot. She spoke with reverence about Susan B. Anthony, Gloria Steinem, Billie Jean King, and other leaders of the women's movement. My mother pulled my sister Lori and me out of school in 1984 to take us to see Geraldine Ferraro speak in front of Oakland City Hall when she was the first female vice presidential candidate representing a major American political party. In my work now, as the father of two young women, and based on my values and worldview, I spend a lot of time thinking about gender dynamics and equality. And yet I was completely caught off guard to see Michelle and all of those other women in that room raise their hands to acknowledge that they had felt physically unsafe in the past 24 hours. It was a specific and poignant example of my own blind spots and the reality that we don't all see things and move through the world the same way.

Our experiences in life and at work can be quite different based on our age, race, gender, orientation, culture, socioeconomic background, language, physical ability, and more. Based on these differences, as well as our values, beliefs, opinions, and worldviews, we often don't see things the same way at all, which can make talking about issues of diversity, inclusion, and belonging challenging. And, coming up with specific ideas, actions, and approaches for addressing these things in a productive and practical way on our teams and in our organizations can be even harder.

We're all biased. There are two types of biases: conscious bias (also known as explicit bias) and unconscious bias (also known as implicit bias). It's important to remember that biases, conscious or unconscious, are not limited to race and ethnicity. Biases may exist toward any social group. Our age, gender, religion, orientation, weight, and many other characteristics are subject to bias.

Unconscious biases are social stereotypes about certain groups of people that we form outside of our own conscious awareness. We all have unconscious beliefs about other people, and these biases stem from our brain's almost automatic process of rapid social categorization, whereby we quickly sort people into groups in our minds. Unconscious bias is far more prevalent than conscious bias and is often incompatible with our values. Certain scenarios can activate our unconscious attitudes and beliefs, like when we're overly stressed, multitasking, in a conflict, scared, feel threatened, or working under significant time pressure. What makes unconscious bias so tricky and potentially damaging is that we aren't aware of it.

A study conducted at Yale University consisted of two versions of the same résumé—identical, except for the candidate's first name (one male, one female)—being given to recruiters. The "male" candidate was regarded as more experienced and gifted, as well as more likely to get hired and given a higher salary.

Another study published in *The Economic Journal* out of the University of Oxford found that eBay auctions of the exact same product received 21 percent more offers when the product was held in a white hand in the photo than when it was held in a black hand.

Our conscious and unconscious biases get in the way of our ability to see each other clearly; have real, open, and authentic discussions about inclusion and belonging; and can perpetuate separation, disconnection, and a lack of trust. We also tend to think of bias in very negative terms, so we can have a hard time fully acknowledging, understanding, and knowing what to do with our biases— often denying that we even have them to begin with.

We have a hard time owning our privilege. Similar to bias, we all have privilege, some of us more than others, but for a number of reasons many of us have an even harder time acknowledging and owning our privilege. It has become almost a slur, or even an outright attack to be called "privileged." In our current social and political climate, there has been a lot of discussion about white privilege and male privilege specifically. A simple Google search of the word *privilege* comes back with this definition: "A special right, advantage, or immunity granted or available only to a particular person or group." The synonyms listed are *advantage, right, benefit, prerogative, entitlement, birthright,* and *due.*

In a larger culture that aspires to values such as hard work, fairness, opportunity, and meritocracy—and given some of the societal dynamics at play in recent years— it's understandable that privilege can be seen in such a negative light and why many of us have a hard time owning our privilege. In some cases, we even argue that we don't or try to hide that we do. However, the bigger issue is being able to realize that we're not all starting at the same place and it's not a level playing field. Some of us simply have advantages that others don't, and in many cases there's not much we can do about them—they're literally based on where we were born and what we look like. But it's important to be able to see that these things exist and to try to understand the impact they have on us and others, all the way around.

A few years ago, a high school teacher posted anonymously on a site called Bored Panda about an important lesson on privilege he shared with his students. He wrote:

> I place a trash can in the front of the room, and have my students take out a piece of paper and crumble it into a ball. I then ask them to try to shoot their paper ball into the trash can from where they're seated. I explain to them first that they as a class represent the country's population, and that the trash can represents America's upper class. Being that we live in the "land of opportunity," everyone will be given the chance to "make it big" and become wealthy by throwing their paper ball into the trash can. Whoever successfully shoots their ball into the trash has made it to the upper class.

Most likely, my students sitting all the way in the back of the classroom will start complaining, saying that their peers sitting in the front have an unfair advantage. I use this opportunity to make the perfect segue into talking about privilege and inequality. The closer you are to the trash can, the better odds you have, the more privilege you have. It's not impossible for those in the back to also shoot their paper balls into the trash can, but it's a lot harder for them.

I make a point to explain that the students sitting in the front row were probably unaware of their privilege initially as they only saw the 10 feet between themselves and their goal. I also point out that the people who were complaining *were* the students sitting in the back. I wrap up the lesson by stating that education is also a privilege, and that my students are capable of using that privilege in order to advocate for those who are behind them.

I love this simple yet powerful example of privilege. With respect to inclusion and belonging, our privilege often gets in our way of noticing, seeing, and understanding certain things, as well as our willingness to engage and take action to make necessary adjustments and changes. In her Netflix special *The Call to Courage*, Brené Brown says, "To not have the conversations (about inclusivity, equity, and diversity) because they make you uncomfortable is the definition of privilege." One of the realities of being in a dominant or majority group of any kind is that often we aren't necessarily forced to think about, talk about, or address these issues. And because they can be scary, difficult, and messy to deal with, we either choose to opt out or we simply don't pay attention. More deeply and even scarier to admit is that sometimes we don't want to acknowledge or let go of our privilege because we're worried about losing it, and afraid of what increased access and opportunity for others might mean to our own ability to succeed.

Our privilege itself and then the denial of the privilege we have are both things that make having authentic conversations about diversity difficult and make it challenging for us to do what needs to be done to create environments of real inclusion and belonging.

We don't feel safe enough to bring our whole selves to work. Over the past few years as I've been traveling around the country and the world talking about my book *Bring Your Whole Self to Work*, I've had people say to me on a number of occasions something to this effect, "Mike, it's much easier for you to bring your whole self to work and to be vulnerable—you're white, straight, male, and have certain advantages and privileges."

When I first heard this, I got a bit defensive—like when Rosie accused me of "mansplaining." However, as I've thought about it more and engaged in this specific discussion with many people, leaders, and groups, I've come to some deeper understandings. Of course, being in the majority and a member of various dominant social groups does provide me with privilege, as we've just been discussing. And yes, in many situations and environments, it's likely easier for me to lower the waterline on my iceberg, be authentic, and bring my whole self to work. However, in my own personal experience of this, I've never found it to be super easy. And in my research, I've come across a concept that speaks to this dynamic specifically: *covering*.

As I talked about in *Bring Your Whole Self to Work*, the term *covering* was coined by sociologist Erving Goffman to describe how even individuals with known stigmatized identities make "a great effort to keep their stigma from looming large." Kenji Yoshino, a constitutional law professor at New York University, developed this idea further and came up with four categories in which we "cover":

1. Appearance
2. Affiliation
3. Advocacy
4. Association

In essence, we often do what we can to cover aspects of ourselves that we believe might put us out of the mainstream of our environment. Yoshino partnered with Christie Smith, managing principal of the Deloitte University Leadership Center for Inclusion, to measure the prevalence of covering at work. They distributed a survey to employees in organizations across 10 industries worldwide. The 3,129 respondents included a mix of ages, genders, races, ethnicities, and orientations. They also represented different levels of seniority within their organizations. Sixty-one percent of respondents reported covering at least one of these four categories at work. According to the study, 83 percent of LGBTQ individuals, 79 percent of blacks, 67 percent of women of color, 66 percent of women, and 63 percent of Hispanics cover.

While the researchers found that covering occurred more frequently within groups that have been historically underrepresented, they also found that 45 percent of straight white men reported covering.

What this research points to is that while it may be easier for some of us to bring our whole selves to work, based on our race, gender, orientation, and other aspects of who we are, it's challenging for all of us. Due to the tendency we all have to cover and the fact that those from specific underrepresented groups are even more likely to cover, understandably, the environment we create on our team and in our organization has a lot to do with this. The amount of psychological safety, modeling from leaders, and social encouragement to be our true selves at work are all factors in our ability to engage with one another authentically. The reason the first pillar we discussed in this book is about creating psychological safety is because that has to come first. Before we're able to engage in conversations about inclusion and create an environment of belonging, we have to feel safe enough to do so. And since creating psychological safety can be challenging in itself, addressing issues of inclusion and creating true belonging can be difficult as well.

These and other things can make talking about issues of race, gender, orientation, age, culture, diversity, and more, hard. They also can get in the way of us taking meaningful action toward creating inclusive environments where everyone feels as though they truly belong. And as we addressed in the previous chapter, these challenges are not excuses; they're just some of the key dynamics that can get in the way.

For team members and leaders within organizations to be able to talk about, address, and instigate positive change in this regard, it takes real courage, commitment, and dedication. Inclusion and belonging are fundamental to the success of your team and company.

The Importance of Inclusion

As we've discussed, inclusion is about understanding and appreciating the differences of the people on our team and in the organization, as well as involving everyone's ideas and perspectives. While this is clearly easier said than done, it's fundamental to creating a culture of high performance, trust, and belonging—which is what will allow your team to thrive. A study conducted by global research analyst Josh Bersin found that inclusive companies had a 2.3 times higher cash flow per employee over the three-year period of the study. And the Deloitte University Leadership Center for Inclusion, in conjunction with the Billie Jean King Leadership Initiative, conducted an extensive survey in which 80 percent of respondents said that inclusion was important in choosing an employer, 39 percent said they would leave their current company for a more inclusive one, and 23 percent said they have already left an organization for a more inclusive one in the past.

Bottom line: Inclusion matters to creating a strong culture, to attracting and retaining the best talent, and to performing at the highest level. To have the greatest impact on the inclusiveness of your team, it's important to focus on emotional intelligence, social intelligence, and cultural intelligence. Let's look at what each of these three things are and why they're so important to inclusion.

Emotional Intelligence

Emotional intelligence, also known as emotional quotient or EQ, is fundamental to our ability to communicate, connect, collaborate, influence, lead, and navigate so many important dynamics, relationships, and aspects of work and life. There are four components of emotional intelligence: self-awareness, self-management, social awareness, and relationship management.

1. **Self-awareness** is about being able to recognize, experience, and understand our own thoughts, feelings, and physical sensations.

2. **Self-management** is about being able to *manage* these thoughts and feelings as best we can, as well as to motivate and discipline ourselves. Self-awareness and self-management are intricately connected.

3. **Social awareness** is about paying attention to other people and tapping into what's going on for them emotionally. Of course, we can't read their minds or feel their feelings, but we can pay attention to others with curiosity, empathy, and interest.

4. **Relationship management** is about how we engage with and relate to other people, and how we manage the different relationships we have. This is also about building trust, connecting, and motivating others. Similar to the first two aspects of EQ, social awareness and relationship management are also closely related.

Our EQ comes into play quite a bit with respect to inclusion. Being more inclusive in how we think, communicate, and act starts with self-awareness and self-management. The more aware we are of our thoughts and feelings, and the more ability we have to manage them effectively, the better we'll be at making important adjustments with respect to inclusivity. Through social awareness and relationship management we can pay more attention to how others are thinking and feeling, as well as notice the impact of our words and actions, and take in essential feedback (both explicitly and implicitly) from those around us about how to operate in the most inclusive and effective way possible.

Social Intelligence

Social intelligence (SI), also referred to as social quotient (SQ), is essentially the ability to get along well with others and to get them to cooperate with us. Sometimes thought of simplistically as "people skills," social intelligence includes an awareness of situations and the social dynamics that govern them, as well as a knowledge of interaction styles and strategies that can help us achieve our objectives in dealing with others. It also involves a certain amount of self-insight and a consciousness of our perceptions and reaction patterns.

Social intelligence consists of two primary components: social awareness and social facility. **Social awareness**, as we just discussed when talking about emotional intelligence, is about having empathy and understanding for the emotions, needs, and concerns of others. It's about being attuned to those around us and empathic to their experience. **Social facility** is about having the interpersonal and communication skills to navigate social and workplace situations effectively. It's also about being able to connect with and influence individuals with diverse backgrounds and groups of all kinds.

The reason social intelligence is so important in regard to inclusion is that it's about being able to mitigate our cognitive biases to improve how we think, act, and react. And what we now know from the study of social neuroscience is that we're wired for connection and there are things we can do to enhance our social intelligence, thus allowing us to connect with anyone, regardless of our differences.

As we've learned over the past decade or two, with the emergence of research in both EQ and SQ, for teams to work well together, communicate effectively, and produce their desired results, enhancing emotional and social intelligence is essential. To create environments of inclusion on our teams, the leader and team members need to leverage and expand these intelligences.

Cultural Intelligence

Cultural intelligence, also known as cultural quotient (CQ), is the ability to relate and work effectively across cultures, and it's essential to inclusion. Although it's less talked about, understood, and researched than EQ and SQ, given the diverse and global nature of business today CQ is becoming increasingly important for people, leaders, and teams who want to thrive.

David Livermore, founder and president of the Cultural Intelligence Center, author of numerous books on CQ including *Leading with Cultural Intelligence*, and one of the world's leading experts on the topic, says, "Cultural intelligence goes beyond existing notions of cultural sensitivity and awareness. It allows you to strategically use cultural differences to come up with more innovative solutions."

David and his team at the Cultural Intelligence Center describe four capabilities that have emerged from their research over the past decade or so: drive, knowledge, strategy, and action.

1. **Drive** has to do with our interest, curiosity, and confidence in multicultural environments and diverse situations. It's about our desire to engage, learn, and connect with people who are different than we are.

2. **Knowledge** is our understanding of how cultures are similar and different. It's about learning as much as we possibly can about cultural differences.

3. **Strategy** is our awareness and ability to plan for multicultural interactions. It's about thinking about and preparing ourselves to be mindful in diverse cultural environments.

4. **Action** is our ability to adapt when relating and working in multicultural contexts. It's about having a flexible repertoire of verbal, nonverbal, and behavioral responses that suit a variety of diverse situations.

Expanding our cultural intelligence is about having curiosity and a genuine desire to learn, a willingness to adapt, and being mindful about how we approach people and situations when our cultural backgrounds differ. This is becoming even more important in business today and is something that we can all continually focus on in our growth and development. Cultural intelligence is also essential to our ability to create a culture of inclusion and belonging on our team and in our organization.

When I spoke with Jennifer Brown, an expert in diversity and inclusion and the author of *How to Be an Inclusive Leader*, on my podcast, she said, "Inclusion is a new business and leadership competency that's essential for all of us. Based on the implicit bias and blind spots that we all have, it's important for us to be willing to listen, learn, and change. Given that we're all judged in business on our ability to build great products and teams, and deliver results, the more inclusive we are, the more successful we'll be."

Inclusion isn't about political correctness, optics, or simply altering our language; it's about expanding our emotional, social, and cultural intelligences, and that of those around us, in a way that allows everyone to be included and creates an environment where people know they belong, so that our team can truly excel.

Creating an Environment of Belonging

DaVita is an incredibly successful health care company that has built a strong culture in a unique way. The company started in 1992 as Total Renal Care. By the late '90s, it was on the verge of bankruptcy when Kent Thiry was appointed CEO. Kent and his leadership team went to work on transforming the company and uniting their workforce through a mission-and-values-based approach. They changed the name of the company to DaVita, which is an Italian phrase meaning "to give life," and began referring to their company as a "Village," to help create a sense of community.

"At DaVita, we often say that we are a community first and a company second . . . We believe that by caring for each other we can improve health care, grow leaders, and make a real difference in the communities we serve," their website says.

DaVita has also been a real leader in diversity, inclusion, and belonging. In 2017 it launched the Executive Inclusion Council to help create a strategy for diversity and inclusion for all of its teammates. In 2018 the company was named to the Bloomberg Gender-Equality Index, which recognizes global organizations for their work advancing gender equality.

Eric Severson, whom I mentioned earlier in this chapter, was DaVita's chief people officer from early 2017 through late 2019. Eric and his team made a commitment to focusing on the importance of belonging.

When I spoke to him on my podcast about this in early 2019, he said, "We want all teammates to think, *this is a place where I belong*. We made an intentional shift from inclusion to belonging. When we focus on inclusion, as important as it is, it can seem like there are insiders and outsiders, and that the outsiders should be 'included.' In our village, everyone is an insider and everyone belongs."

DaVita is one of many companies on the leading edge of building a culture of belonging. And, as Eric alluded to and we've been discussing throughout this chapter, while inclusion is essential for so many reasons, what we truly want to create is an environment where *everyone* belongs. Eric, who is gay, also said, "Most of us who self-identify as part of a minority group would rather be included in what the majority is doing, than excluded. But, we'd rather all just know that we belong here."

According to another study conducted by Deloitte in 2017 called Unleashing the Power of Inclusion, 80 percent of people said that belonging is important when choosing an employer and 62 percent of people said that they would leave (or have already left) their organization for one that emphasizes belonging more. Creating an environment of belonging is about making it safe for people to bring their whole selves to work, honoring and appreciating everyone on the team, and remembering that our desire to belong is universal.

Belonging Is a Fundamental Human Need

Psychologist Abraham Maslow studied human development and came up with a theory of motivation based on five fundamental needs we all have as human beings. Maslow's well-known hierarchy of needs is often displayed as a pyramid, with the largest, most fundamental needs at the bottom. The crux is that our most basic needs must be met before we become motivated to achieve higher levels. The five needs Maslow describes, from the bottom of the pyramid to the top are:

1. Physiological. These are biological requirements for human survival, such as air, food, drink, shelter, clothing, warmth, and sleep. If these needs are not satisfied, the human body cannot function optimally. Maslow considered physiological needs the most important, as all the other needs become secondary until these needs are met.

2. Safety. These needs are about protection from the elements, security, order, law, stability, and more. This is also about feeling safe physically, mentally, and emotionally, as well as having enough work, money, and resources to care for ourselves and our family.

3. Belonging. After our physiological and safety needs have been fulfilled, the third level of human need is social and involves feelings of belongingness. The need for interpersonal relationships motivates behavior. Some examples include friendship, trust, acceptance, and receiving and giving love. Belonging is also about affiliation and being part of a group or community (whether it's family, friends, work, or some other team). After knowing that we can survive and that we're safe, we have a need to feel we belong.

4. Esteem. Maslow described our need for esteem as two types. One is esteem we have for ourselves (achievement, dignity, confidence, independence). The second is respect from others or reputation (status, attention, recognition, prestige).

5. Self-Actualization. This is about realizing our personal potential, experiencing self-fulfillment, and seeking personal growth. Maslow described this need as a desire "to become everything one is capable of becoming."

Based on Maslow's hierarchy, we can see that belonging is something we all want and need as human beings. It doesn't matter where we come from, how old we are, our gender, our sexual orientation, our race, our ethnicity, our physical size or ability, our socioeconomic status, our religion, or anything else about us, the need to belong is essential and universal.

And while it is true that certain groups of people have been and continue to be underrepresented in particular environments, which is why diversity and inclusion continue to be so important, focusing on belonging is fundamental. Regardless of our background or identity, we've all experienced both belonging and not belonging. When we experience being an "outsider" in a situation or group, it triggers our brain to release cortisol, the stress hormone. However, when we feel like we belong, our brain and nervous system feel safe, releasing oxytocin, which increases our sense of connection to others, reduces our anxiety, and promotes our well-being.

Ernst & Young conducted its first "Belonging Barometer" study in 2018 and found that when people feel like they belong, they are more productive, motivated, and engaged, as well as 3.5 times more likely to contribute their full innovative potential. According to the study, 56 percent of the people surveyed felt they belong most at work when they feel trusted and respected, 39 percent of people said having the ability to speak freely and voice their opinions contributed to their sense of belonging, and 34 percent said that when their unique contributions are valued, they feel like they belong. A study conducted by the University of Iowa found that a sense of belonging and attachment to a group of co-workers is a better motivator for some employees than money.

Chip Conley is the author of a number of best-selling books including *Peak: How Great Companies Get Their Mojo from Maslow*. At age 26, he founded Joie de Vivre Hospitality (JdV), transforming an inner-city motel into the second-largest boutique hotel brand in America. He sold JdV after running it as CEO for 24 years, and soon the founders of Airbnb asked him to help transform their promising start-up into the world's leading hospitality brand. Chip served as Airbnb's head of global hospitality and strategy for four years and today acts as the company's strategic advisor for hospitality and leadership. When I talked to

Chip about the importance of belonging, he said, "Another reason why 'belonging' is growing in importance in companies is because it's not the exclusive scope of the HR team and it's not something one does just to be politically correct. Unfortunately, diversity and inclusion can seem that way for some people. But belonging is something everyone in the company can do in small ways every day."

As a successful business leader and thought leader who is passionate about customer experience, company culture, and conscious capitalism, Chip played a key role in helping influence Airbnb's brand and culture approach. A year or so after Chip came on board, Airbnb launched its new brand, logo, and tagline of "Belong Anywhere." Chip said, "I joined in April 2013 and a month later helped facilitate our Exec Committee's all-day retreat, which is when the idea of 'Belong Anywhere' started to take root. Those two words were powerful as a brand because no other hospitality company had staked out this territory of how customers can feel they 'belong' and our hosts, of course, were 'anywhere,' because there are homes everywhere. We then started to create internal employee programs and gave 'belo' (shorthand for 'belonging') awards to employees in our 21 global offices who most exemplified a 'belong anywhere' way of being in their office. I do believe that this internal mantra of 'belong anywhere' had a positive impact on the team and the culture. We received the award for the best place to work in the U.S. by Glassdoor in 2016."

Belonging is about making sure that everyone is not only included, but also feels safe, appreciated, and honored as a full and important member of the team. In other words, belonging is about remembering that we're all in this together.

The Leader's Role in Inclusion and Belonging

Leaders play a significant role in creating environments of inclusion and belonging within teams and organizations. According to author and leadership expert Nilofer Merchant, "If there is one thing any leader can do to create more innovation, it's to lead in such a way as to create belonging."

Whether you're in a senior leadership role, you manage a small team, or you simply want to influence those around you, here are some specific things you can do as a leader that contribute to the culture of inclusion and belonging in your group and your company:

Acknowledge your bias and privilege. As we discussed earlier in this chapter, we all have bias and privilege. And, although some of us have more of this than others, it's important for leaders to be able to acknowledge their own bias and privilege, first and foremost to themselves, and also, if they're courageous enough, to their teams. An essential aspect of moving beyond bias—both explicit and implicit—is being aware of it to the best of our ability. And understanding the privilege that we have, in general and specifically as leaders, can allow us to connect more deeply with the people on our teams, have more empathy for their experience, and enhance both inclusion and belonging. Taking or deepening our training in implicit bias and becoming more conscious of the privileges we have, without shame, are essential aspects of inclusive leadership.

Get specific feedback, advice, and education. As leaders in today's global business world we're constantly facing new challenges, ideas, and people. It's difficult to keep up with everything and the rapid pace of change. With respect to diversity, inclusion, and belonging, there is so much new research and data, as well as new concepts, terms, and ideas coming forward all the time. (Not to mention the fact that even with the best of intentions, we all have blind spots.) So, it's important to get as much feedback, advice, and education as we can, and to do this in an ongoing way. This is one of the most important leadership competencies these days, and some of us haven't had much helpful training, experience, or feedback in this regard. Soliciting ideas and input from experts, people who are different than we are, and other leaders, are all things we can do to learn. Being open to the advice of those who are courageous enough to speak up, without getting defensive, is essential. Also crucial to this effort is our willingness to listen, learn, and get educated, especially about issues and dynamics that may not specifically relate to us and our background but do relate to others on our team and in our company.

Be mindful of your language. Diversity, inclusion, and belonging aren't just about language, although language plays a big role. There are lots of trigger words that can cause people to feel excluded and even offended. The most acceptable and inclusive language is constantly changing, so it's important to keep up on this as best we can and to ask for advice or feedback if we're not clear. We're going to make mistakes with our language, despite our good intentions. If we're mindful both of what we're saying and where it's coming from, we can make sure the things we say aren't excluding or upsetting people, consciously or unconsciously, and that we're doing what we can with our words to have those on our team feel as included as possible.

It's also important for us to be aware of microaggressions—things we (or others) may do or say, intentionally or unintentionally, that cause people to feel excluded. Rosie pointing out my "mansplaining" was both an example of me being self-righteous and of my microaggression toward Michelle (acting as though I was being helpful, when, really, I was just trying to prove I was right and my approach to parking the car was superior).

Being aware of terms and language used (or not used) to talk about certain people, traits, and groups is important. For example, a few years ago I kept hearing the term *cisgender* but was afraid to ask what it meant. When I finally asked and found out that it meant our sense of personal identity and gender corresponds to our birth sex, it made sense to me. It's essentially the opposite of transgender. I started referring to myself as a cisgender man, which gave me more awareness in this regard, and also allowed me to communicate with others in a way that is more inclusive of gender identity variance. I also added my preferred pronouns (he/him/his) to my e-mail signature as a way of acknowledging this and being more inclusive to others.

Mentor and sponsor people. One of the most impactful things we can do as leaders is to mentor and sponsor people on our team and in our organization. However, sometimes we use these words interchangeably, when they are actually distinct. When we *mentor* someone, we advise them, coach them, and share our wisdom, experience, and knowledge with them in a way that we hope can benefit them personally and professionally. When we *sponsor* someone, we mentor them and we also *advocate* for them. This might mean we tell other leaders about them, vouch for them, and use our privilege, influence, and position to support their success. Of course, not everyone gets mentored and sponsored in the same way, just like not everyone gets promoted. It's important to be mindful of this dynamic so that we're not intentionally excluding people in the process.

When we're willing to mentor and sponsor people who might not otherwise gain visibility or access, it makes a huge difference. According to the Center for Talent Innovation, a New York-based nonprofit that advises companies on diversity and inclusion, 71 percent of mentors say that their chosen mentees are the same race and gender as they are. As leaders we're in positions to mentor and sponsor people and thus create growth and opportunities for them. When we're willing to be generous with our mentorship and sponsorship, and we do this for a diverse group of people, it can have a real positive impact on the inclusion and sense of belonging that exists within our team and company.

Know the differences of diversity, inclusion, and belonging . . . and focus on all three. As we discussed earlier in the chapter, diversity is about expanded representation in our groups and organizations of people from different backgrounds, inclusion is about appreciating all of these differences and making sure we do all that we can to not exclude people, and belonging is about creating an environment where everyone, whether they're in a dominant or nondominant group, feels like they matter and that they're a full, equal, and important member of the group. All three things are really important. And as leaders, it's essential to understand their differences and to focus on all three. Paying attention to the diversity (or lack thereof) on the team and making sure the pipeline is filled with a diverse group of applicants for jobs and promotions are two of the most essential things that leaders can focus on in this regard. Doing all we can to make sure that differences are understood, respected, and appreciated, and that no one feels excluded, is fundamental to inclusion. And making sure everyone on the team feels a true sense of belonging is critical.

The Team Member's Role in Inclusion and Belonging

Everyone on the team and in the organization plays an important role in creating an environment of inclusion and belonging. This is not just the job of senior leaders, the person we report to, or the HR team. Even if your role involves you managing people or other managers, or you happen to work in a specific function that focuses on these issues directly, we're all members of a team and individual members of the company. Each of the suggestions listed above about what leaders can do also applies to team members, and there are some additional things to think about and do as a member of your team that can positively influence the culture of inclusion and belonging around you.

Speak up. While it can be scary and has a lot to do with how much psychological safety we feel, one of the most important things for us to do as team members is speak up. As the saying goes, "If you see something, say something." This means that if something is done or said that makes you feel uncomfortable or excluded, let someone know in a proactive way. Also, if you see or hear something that you think might be upsetting, offensive, or problematic in terms of inclusion and belonging, be willing to bring that up as well. This may involve a direct conversation with a co-worker, manager, or someone else with whom you work. If you don't feel safe enough to bring this up directly, maybe there is someone you can talk to about it who could bring it up on your behalf. Not saying something or simply complaining about it, while understandable and normal, won't make things better.

Call people in (not out). Oftentimes when we see something we deem problematic, unfair, or offensive with respect to diversity, inclusion, and belonging, and we have the courage to speak up about it, there's a tendency to call people out. In other words, we point out what we perceive as their misstep or misdeed. Of course, there's an important place for this on our teams and in our society at large, and yet, what will usually be most productive and conducive to building and maintaining a culture of inclusion and belonging is for us to call each other *in*, not *out*. Calling someone in is about removing our self-righteousness, along with as much of our animosity as possible. It's really about being authentic (honest, without self-righteousness, and with vulnerability) in our communication and feedback.

Calling in comes from a place of truth and compassion, as well as with a desire to inform, educate, enlighten, and engage in important discussions. In some cases, we can call people in while we're together in a group setting. In other cases, it might be more appropriate for us to have this type of conversation one-on-one. We can use our EQ and SQ to determine what we think will be most effective in each situation.

Ask for what you want. One of my favorite sayings is "The answer is always no if you don't ask." So often there are things we see that we think should be different. Or there are things we want that would make us feel more included and create a greater sense of belonging. But, for a number of reasons, we don't feel comfortable or confident enough to ask for them. When we ask for what we want, we put ourselves out there and risk being rejected, judged, ridiculed, or excluded. However, when we have the courage to ask for what we want, three things can happen.

First, we might actually get what we want. Second, we let the people around us and those on our team know what's important to us. Third, we practice being vulnerable with one another, which can make things safer, connect us to each other, and ultimately deepen our sense of belonging.

Asking for what we want is one of the best ways we can use our voice and it's an effective way to create positive change. Similar to speaking up, if, for whatever reason, we don't feel safe enough to ask for what we want, maybe we can ask someone else to ask on our behalf in a way that might be well-received.

Bring your whole self to work. The more willing we are to show up authentically, lower the waterline on our iceberg, and bring our whole selves to work, the more likely the people around us will do the same. As we discussed earlier in this chapter, all of us, regardless of our race, gender, orientation, or background have a tendency to "cover." This keeps us disconnected from one another and reinforces the notion of insiders and outsiders. And, as we talked about in the previous chapter on psychological safety, being authentic not only liberates us, it also encourages the people on our team and those around us to do the same. The more courageous we are to be ourselves, share ourselves, and express ourselves, the safer it becomes for everyone and the more conducive the team becomes for inclusion and belonging.

Be curious and open. Curiosity is powerful. When we're curious, we're open-minded; willing to learn; and fascinated by new ideas, unique experiences, and people who may be different than we are. The more willing we are to be curious and open, the more we can learn about the people on our team, their different cultures and backgrounds, and how they experience things in their own unique way. Furthermore, curiosity makes us much less defensive. Even if we feel awkward or uncomfortable, asking people questions, respectfully, about aspects of cultural difference can open up really interesting and important conversations. This allows us to learn, grow, and connect, as well as find common ground with one another. Similarly, being open about our own backgrounds and aspects of ourselves makes it easier for us to talk about these things as a group and makes these issues less taboo.

What Your Team Can Do to Create a Culture of Inclusion and Belonging

Whether it's the team you manage, the team you're a member of, or both, there are some specific things you can think about, talk about, and do as a group to enhance your culture of inclusion and belonging. Here are some ideas:

Share your diversity stories with one another. We all have a "diversity story." Clearly anyone who self-identifies as a member of one or more minority groups has had a lot of experience dealing with their race, gender, orientation, or other aspects of their identity and background. Those of us, like me, who are members of nonminority groups often don't think we have much to say or share in this regard. However, if we're each willing to lower the waterline on our iceberg—specifically with respect to diversity, inclusion, and belonging—we find that we all have thoughts, ideas, feelings, and experiences we can share. Every single one of us has experienced feeling different, like an outsider, and a lack of belonging at certain times in our lives. Clearly some of us have experienced this more than others, and in some cases in really painful and scary ways. The more willing we are to be real and vulnerable about these experiences, whatever they may be, the more empathy and understanding we can have for one another. Sharing a bit about your experiences growing up and your family background can also help your teammates understand you better. Your team can do the "If you really knew me . . . " exercise on pages 30–31, specifically focused on telling your diversity stories and sharing your authentic feelings and experience of being who you are in terms of race, gender, orientation, and anything else.

Have compassion for each other. One of the best things we can do as a team is have compassion for one another, in general, and especially as it relates to inclusion and belonging. These issues are sensitive, and they run deep for many of us, making them difficult to talk about and address in a meaningful and productive way. However, if we engage in these things with compassion, and give people the benefit of the doubt, we'll almost always be more effective in how we address them. If we're able to talk about these issues more compassionately, it can allow us to come up with new ideas, suggestions, and solutions that can enhance the inclusion and belonging of our team and organization. The notion of assuming positive intent is really important in general, and especially when we're dealing with important discussions and dynamics like these.

Be willing to talk about these things authentically. Our willingness to address these sensitive topics with authenticity as a team, can bring us closer together and allow us to truly create a culture of inclusion and belonging. The paradox is that we have to do more than just talk—we have to act. However, if we can't talk about these things in a real way, it's almost impossible to take any meaningful action to create more inclusion and belonging. The more vulnerable we are and the less defensive we get, the better off we'll be.

Learn together. Learning and development is important for our success—as individuals, as leaders, and as teams. Specifically with respect to diversity, inclusion, and belonging, when we learn about these things together, it creates a safer environment to listen to each other, learn from one another, and grow together—individually and collectively. Having the team go through trainings on unconscious bias and other related topics is essential. And creating opportunities for the team to continue to learn as much as possible about diversity, inclusion, and belonging will allow us to more deeply understand and embody their importance.

Find common ground. As we talked about in the previous chapter, the deeper down below the waterline we go, the more similar we become. One of the paradoxes of diversity is that while we're all quite different on the surface— both in how look or where we come from, as well as our personalities and perspectives—we also share so much common ground as human beings. We all experience joy, pain, love, sadness, gratitude, fear, happiness, anger, and everything in between. We all have people we love, care about, and worry about. Each of us grew up with unique family experiences, although when we open up about these things we often find some similarities. The more we can focus on finding common ground, the more we can engage in ways that have us experience belonging, which is universal and fundamental to all of us.

Thinking about, talking about, addressing, and looking at ways to impact our team and organization positively in terms of diversity, inclusion, and belonging isn't easy. These things can be confusing, painful, frustrating, and emotional. As excited as I am to write and talk about these issues in this book and in my work, I found researching and writing this chapter to be both enlightening and scary all at the same time. It's essential for us to have compassion for each other, as I just mentioned, and also for ourselves as we engage in these important and emotionally charged topics.

If we're willing to be honest with ourselves, real with each other, and to do the hard and important work that must be done—personally and collectively—we can create a strong culture of inclusion and belonging on our team that will allow us all to thrive. To do this, we have to remember that we are, in fact, all in this thing together. As I mentioned in the Introduction, there is no *them*, it's all *us*.

EMBRACE SWEATY-PALMED CONVERSATIONS

I was on a plane a few years ago flying from Fort Lauderdale to New York. I'd spoken at two events in south Florida, was flying up to New York for some meetings, then on to Boston for another event, and then back to Florida for my final event before heading home. It was a crazy but exciting week. I was in full-on work/travel mode, which means I had tunnel vision—focused just on getting to where I needed to get to, taking care of myself physically so I'd be ready to go when it was time to speak, and getting as much work done as possible while on my flights and in my hotel rooms.

I was working on my laptop even as people were still boarding the plane that afternoon. Sitting on the aisle, I had to get up when the two people who were in the window and middle seat came to sit down. I greeted them briefly. They were together—a man who looked to be in his mid-50s and a woman who looked to be close to 80, whom I assumed was his mother.

As the flight began to take off, I had to put my computer away and wait for the plane to get to 10,000 feet before I could start working again, so I started flipping channels on the live TV in front of me. I landed on CNN and was catching up on the news of the day. We reached 10,000 feet and I pulled my laptop out and began to work. I had e-mails to catch up on and I was reviewing my latest podcast episode—so I pulled my headphones out of the airplane armrest and plugged them into my computer.

About 10 minutes later, out of the corner of my eye, I saw the man sitting to my right in the window seat motioning toward the TV screen in front of me. It was still showing CNN, but I wasn't paying attention to it and couldn't hear it since my headphones were plugged into my laptop. Then I heard him say, "Fake news, fake news!" I wasn't sure if he was talking to me, to his mom, or just talking out loud to himself. So, I ignored him and kept working. Then he did it again, this time more demonstratively, his voice getting louder as he pointed at the screen.

I stopped what I was doing, took out my ear buds, turned to him, and asked, "Are you talking to me?"

"Yes! CNN is fake news. It's just a bunch of liberal propaganda."

I was a bit taken aback by his intensity. He seemed angry, and I wasn't sure what to do. I felt nervous, but also intrigued. He and his mom both had the TVs in front of them turned to Fox News. I said, "I notice you're watching Fox."

"It's the only honest news on TV," he said passionately.

At this moment I realized I had a choice. There were various ways I could avoid getting into an argument with him. I also had a ton of work that I needed to get done. But my heart and mind were racing—I felt scared and defensive, but also excited and curious. I wanted to see where this conversation might go and what might happen, so I said, "Well, I'd be careful if I were you. I've read some studies that say people who consistently watch Fox are the most misinformed news viewers in America." As you can imagine, he didn't appreciate this comment.

"Oh, I see, you're one of those liberal elites who thinks he knows everything."

And then we were off to the races from there. We argued about Donald Trump, Barack Obama, Hillary Clinton, immigration, the economy, climate change, the military, guns, the police, and a number of other issues. I tried to stay calm and not get defensive, but that didn't work so well. He continued to call me names and it got heated.

It was an odd and interesting experience to find myself in a pretty aggressive debate with this man whom I hadn't known an hour before. And while I wasn't concerned for my safety in any way, I did find it uncomfortable and upsetting. I also didn't really enjoy being called "wimpy," "whiney," "snowflake," and other things.

As the conversation escalated, I finally said, "Stop! Look, we clearly disagree in some pretty fundamental ways about these issues. But my deeper concern is that here we are, two strangers sitting on an airplane, and you're calling me names simply because we disagree about politics."

Then I shifted gears completely and asked him a question. "Do you have children?" He looked at me with surprise and said, "What?"

"Do you have kids?" I asked again.

"Yes," he said. "I have four."

"Wow," I said. "That's great. We have two young daughters."

"We have two boys and two girls," he said. "Our oldest is thirty and the other three are in their twenties."

"So you've been at the parenting thing much longer than I have," I said. "I worry sometimes that I'm doing things (or not doing things) that might be messing up our girls. I try to do the best I can, but sometimes I wonder if I'm doing a good job as a father." Then I asked him, "Do you ever worry about that, or did you when your kids were younger?"

He paused, looked at me in a different way than he'd been looking at me, and didn't answer the question initially. Eventually he said, "Of course. I think every parent feels that way at some point."

"I suppose you're right," I said. "Maybe, just like as a father I try to do the best I can and think my ideas, decisions, and actions are right, with respect to some of these big political issues, I have strong opinions, but I'm not sure I know what the solutions are. Some of these challenges are so large and complex, it's possible that the answers are much bigger and more involved than I can even understand."

At this moment, he was looking at me like I was a little crazy, but there seemed to be some recognition of what I was saying in his eyes. He said, "I guess?"

We both laughed a little, there was an awkward silence between us, and after almost 45 minutes of arguing, we just stopped. I went back to my laptop and he went back to chatting softly with his mom.

As my heart rate came down and I sat there reflecting on the intense conversation that had just taken place, a few thoughts came to mind. First of all, I had no idea if either of us convinced the other of *anything*. I didn't walk away agreeing with his ideas or political views, and I doubt he did with mine. However, I did learn a bit more about where he was coming from and felt the anger, fear, and frustration he had about the media, the country, and the state of politics, which was actually enlightening for me on a number of levels. This man who was more than 10 years older than I am, a father of four, and a firefighter from Long Island had a *very* different background and worldview than mine. Second of all, when I was being self-righteous and defensive, it was hard for me to listen, hear, understand, and connect with him in any way. However, when we talked about our children, the conversation got more vulnerable and real, and I was able to find some common ground with him below the waterlines of our icebergs, which allowed us to, momentarily at least, connect with each other—human being to human being, father to father. And in that instant, I felt more empathy, compassion, and understanding for this man sitting across from me, even though we fundamentally disagreed about some pretty important issues.

This situation on the airplane was a bit odd, uncomfortable, and extreme. It's not the normal conversation I have when I'm on a plane or chatting with people I've just met. I did, of course, choose to have the discussion because I was curious and wanted to see what would happen, even though it was a bit scary and awkward. And while arguing about politics on airplanes with strangers may not be all that productive or something we're even interested in doing in our daily lives, with the people we regularly interact with, and especially with our teams at work, there are lots of situations that arise when what's needed is for us to have a tough, but important conversation.

Along these lines, a mentor of mine said something to me years ago that I think about and reference often. "Mike, you know what stands between you and the kind of relationships you really want to have with people? It's probably a 10-minute, sweaty-palmed conversation you're too afraid to have. If you get good at those 10-minute, sweaty-palmed conversations, you'll have fantastic relationships—you'll resolve conflicts, build trust, and be able to work through things," he said. "You'll get to know people who are different from you, you'll talk about important issues that need to be addressed, and you'll be able to give and receive feedback that's necessary to everyone's growth and success. But if you avoid them, as most of us do because they can be hard, uncomfortable, and sometimes messy, you'll simply be a victim of whomever you live with, work with, and interact with in life."

His wisdom was spot on. These sweaty-palmed conversations often involve talking about a touchy subject, engaging in an important debate or conflict, giving or receiving some hard but essential feedback, or some combination of these things. And our ability to engage in these types of conversations effectively as a group has *everything* to do with our team's performance, trust, and culture.

According to Dr. Bernie Mayer, professor of conflict resolution at the Werner Institute at Creighton University and author of *The Conflict Paradox*, healthy conflict is essential for teams to perform their best. "Unless we can empower people to deal with problems that arise along the way, to face difficulties, to recognize and adjust when strategies aren't working or are impossible to implement, to help those who are struggling, to handle the inevitable tensions and conflicts that challenging work engenders, and to maintain a positive attitude about that work, we cannot build a truly effective team, unit or organization," he says. If conflict isn't dealt with directly, he adds, "problems fester, important views are squelched, and effective communication is inhibited."

Our ability to embrace these sweaty-palmed conversations is fundamental to our success—individually and collectively. However, it's not all that easy to do. These challenges often have to do with the social norms and environment in which we work, and they also have to do with how we were raised and what we learned from our very first team (our family). Here are some specific things that get in our way and make it difficult to engage in these important discussions successfully.

We don't feel safe. Talking about sensitive subjects, engaging in debates or conflicts, and exchanging feedback in an effective way all require trust, safety, and a sense of belonging. We focused on trust and psychological safety in the first pillar and on inclusion and belonging in the second pillar because these things are foundational to building strong relationships and teams. Without them, it's difficult, and in some cases seems almost impossible, to embrace sweaty-palmed conversations and talk about things that truly matter. When we don't feel safe, most of our attention is focused on protecting ourselves, which makes it even harder to talk openly about anything controversial, emotional, or sensitive. If we're worried we'll be harshly judged, ridiculed, shamed, kicked out of the group (literally or figuratively), or in any way that there will be negative retribution for speaking up or engaging, we'll often choose not to, or we'll talk about the issue to others in a gossipy way, so as to save face and protect ourselves from real or perceived harm. Not feeling safe makes it really hard to address tough conversations directly.

We aren't all that good at engaging in difficult conversations. Most of us don't have a ton of training, experience, or even know what "success" feels like with these types of discussions. They can be tricky, messy, and awkward. Therefore, we tend to avoid them. We also don't often work on our skills in this regard. When we're forced to have a sweaty-palmed conversation, we tend to grind our way through it and focus mainly on survival. We usually don't think we're very good at them, and in many cases, we aren't. Our fear, discomfort, and difficulty lead to our avoidance, which doesn't allow us to get much better or feel more confident, and it becomes a vicious cycle. While there are some specific skills and techniques we can both use and enhance, being "good" at having these tough conversations is much more about willingness and courage, than ability. And, the more we engage in difficult conversations, the better we get.

We don't want to hurt others or get hurt ourselves. When I ask people what stops them from engaging in conversations like these, one of the answers I hear most often is, "I don't want to hurt other people's feelings." And while I know that's true for most of us, myself included, we've all likely been in situations where we spoke up, told the truth about something, or gave some specific feedback and someone's feelings did, in fact, get hurt. However, many years ago I realized that while I don't particularly like hurting other people's feelings, often my bigger concern is having *my* feelings hurt. It sounds nicer for us to say "I don't want to hurt their feelings," but in reality, what's usually harder for us to deal with is having other people get upset with us. Often this fear has us hold back, avoid, or water down our feedback, input, or the conversations we really need to have. And, in this specific case, when we focus on not wanting to hurt other people, while there is some inherent kindness and care that can be involved, we're often putting the responsibility on them, and not taking personal ownership of the situation. We think to ourselves, *I would be completely open, direct, and authentic, but they're so sensitive and I don't want to hurt them, so I can't.*

We don't want to make things worse. Sometimes having sweaty-palmed conversations doesn't go well. We've all had situations where a conflict existed, and in our attempt to address it not only were we not able to get it resolved, but by bringing it up and talking about it directly, things got *worse*. Understandably, our fear of throwing gasoline on the fire can stop us from engaging. And because of the way our brain and nervous system are wired, we tend to hang on to negative experiences much more strongly than positive ones (our amygdala stores painful memories for self-protection and survival), so we have *physical* reasons, in addition to emotional ones, for not wanting to engage. If we're concerned we'll make the situation worse by addressing it directly, we're much more likely not to talk about it at all or to talk about it to others, which, ironically, almost always does make things worse.

Cultural differences. As we discussed in the previous chapters and we know from experience, significant differences in our backgrounds—especially racial, ethnic, gender, religious, age, orientation, and language differences—can make it challenging to engage in these types of conversations effectively. Even if we share similar backgrounds, the cultures of the family in which we grew up and where we've worked previously often come into play.

89

My wife, Michelle, and I grew up about an hour away from each other. I was in Oakland and she was in Novato, on the other side of the San Francisco Bay, in Marin county. We're both white (my ancestors are mainly from Ireland and Ukraine, and hers are primarily from France, Ireland, and England) and we're close in age. However, we don't communicate the same way and come from families who are quite different in this regard. I learned this in a pretty specific way a few months after Michelle and I started dating in late 2000.

She invited me to dinner at her grandmother's house in San Anselmo—another town in Marin County, south of Novato and north of San Francisco. Her Grandma, whom everyone called Gramita, was the matriarch of the family and was still living in the house that she and her late husband bought when they moved their family to California in the 1940s. I was excited by and grateful for the invitation. And, understandably, I was a little nervous. I had met Michelle's dad, Jerry, and her brother, Steve, individually over those first few months, but I had yet to meet Gramita or any of the other members of the family.

I got to the house that night and was introduced to everyone. They were all very nice and pleasant people, and they seemed happy to meet me. I felt fairly relaxed once I got there. Of course, I wanted to make a good impression and have them like me. Over the course of dinner, we talked about a variety of things and I noticed they seemed a little quiet, but overall, I thought the night went well. I was happy to meet them all and I felt like it was a success.

When Michelle and I got into the car to drive back to San Francisco, I was curious to hear how she thought the evening went . . . and more specifically, how I did meeting her family for the first time.

I said, "So, how do you think that went?"

She paused, and replied, "How did *you* think it went?"

I thought this was a bit of an odd response and it made me a little nervous. I said, "I thought it went pretty well. Your family seems nice. I did notice they didn't talk all that much though."

Then Michelle said, "I know, because you talked the whole time."

"What?" I asked, somewhat surprised by her response.

"In my family, we don't interrupt," she said.

"Oh wow," I replied. "In my family, if you don't interrupt, you don't get to say *anything*."

In my nervousness and wanting to make a good impression, I guess I had been talking a lot. And since they're such polite people who don't interrupt, they just let me go right on talking, which is something I like to do anyway. My fear, insecurity, and desire to impress them probably got in the way of my awareness of what was going on. And since no one was jumping in or interrupting me, I just kept on going.

We laugh about this now, but it was an important lesson for me at the time—both about Michelle's family and also as a reminder that even if we look the same and grow up in the same general area, the culture of our families can be quite different. How we communicate, and especially how we engage in sweaty-palmed conversations, can vary a lot based on our personality, background, culture, and so much more.

These are among the key factors that can make it difficult or challenging to effectively have tough, but important conversations with each other at work and in our teams. As we've discussed in the previous chapters, pointing out some of the dynamics that make something hard isn't necessarily about making excuses, it's more about understanding, acknowledging, and taking ownership of what might get in our way so that we can consciously choose to move *beyond* these things.

Conflict

The ability for you and your team to effectively engage in conflict may not be all that easy or fun, but it is fundamental to your performance, both individually and collectively. When I speak to people, leaders, and teams about this important topic, I often ask, "When you hear the word *conflict*, what comes to mind?"

In response to this, I hear things like, "fight, argument, disagreement, debate, anger, etc." They're likely thinking of a scenario like the one I had with that man on the plane.

However, when I then ask, "What becomes available when we address and resolve a conflict?" people often say, "new ideas, more trust, solutions to problems, understanding, connection," and more.

While most of us don't particularly *enjoy* conflict, we all know how valuable and important it is, especially to our teams, our work, and to building a strong culture and performing at the highest level. It's really about our relationship to conflict and our fear about it that makes it difficult, more so than the conflict itself.

A cross-cultural study conducted by the Institute for Research on Labor and Employment at the University of California, Berkeley, found that conflict is both liberating and fundamental to team success. According to the study, teams that can engage effectively in tough conversations have a significant competitive advantage over their counterparts—generating better ideas, more creativity, and greater innovation.

Clearly it takes courage to have these types of sweaty-palmed conversations (which sometimes take more than 10 minutes, of course) and to engage in conflict directly. It's vulnerable and often frightening for a number of reasons. However, usually what's most at risk is our ego. And although there are no guarantees, most of us have learned the hard way that it's almost always better to address a conflict directly than to avoid it, which usually causes it to fester and get worse. We also know that not being willing to have these types of conversations is ultimately way more damaging to us, our relationships, and our team than taking the risk and engaging.

Embracing conflict in a healthy way is important for us personally and also for our team. It's essential to our ability to connect with each other, understand one another, and create the kinds of solutions, ideas, and outcomes that are necessary for our success. And, if we're in leadership positions and part of a leadership team, engaging in conflict courageously and effectively is not only important for the performance of our team, it also has a critical impact on the culture of the organization.

Divided Together, United Apart

Dan Henkle worked for Gap Inc. for 25 years. He had various roles within human resources and global sustainability, and was the president of the Gap Foundation before leaving the company in 2017. Dan and I had a chance to partner a handful of times, and I was always impressed with his thoughtful approach to leadership and culture. At one point in his career, Dan was the SVP of HR for Old Navy, one of Gap's biggest and most successful brands.

He told me, "Our brand president left somewhat unexpectedly and, it was decided that while the company searched for a permanent replacement instead of putting one person in the role on an interim basis, four of us on the leadership team would report to the Gap Inc. CEO and run the brand as a group. This was both exciting and challenging, as you can imagine. We realized immediately that how we communicated with one another as a group, and how we then communicated with the rest of the leaders and team members within the brand was going to be crucial to our success."

Dan went on to say, "Right away we made a commitment that we'd be willing to be divided when we were together, but we had to be united when we were apart. This meant that we could argue, debate, and hash things out in a real way when we met with each other as a group. But, when we left the room and ended the meeting, we had to be aligned and a united front. We knew that if we didn't do that, especially given the uncertainty of the overall situation—people wondering what was going to happen and when we'd have a new president—that there would be those who wanted to pull each of us in different directions. It wasn't always easy, but I think we did a good job of keeping our commitment of being divided together and united apart, which allowed us to be successful in leading the brand through that transition."

This idea was essential for Dan and his fellow leaders at Old Navy, and it's an approach that's important for *every* team. If we have the courage, willingness, and ability to engage in the sweaty-palmed conversations that need to happen and we do so directly and productively, it not only brings us closer together, it allows us to come up with innovative solutions to the big problems that need our attention and focus. If we do this passionately behind closed doors and we leave the meeting aligned, with a commitment not to throw anyone or the team under the bus, it empowers and emboldens our performance, trust, and culture, and it also models this for the rest of the organization.

Engaging in Healthy Conflict

As important as engaging in conflict is to the culture and performance of a team, there are both healthy and unhealthy ways of doing it. If we've done the important work to create psychological safety, as well as inclusion and belonging, within the team, we're more likely to have a culture that is conducive to healthy debate and disagreement. It's important to be *intentional* about this and to use our EQ and SQ in ways that allow for us to engage in productive sweaty-palmed conversations.

Here are seven things to remember when dealing with a conflict or disagreement—one-on-one, within a group, or within the entire team:

1. Take responsibility. This is not about pointing fingers or figuring out who's at fault; it's about owning up to the situation and recognizing that we're a part of the issue. It's also about owning our emotions and reactions in an authentic, healthy way.

2. Address the conflict directly. Conflicts are always handled most successfully when they're dealt with directly and promptly. Be real and vulnerable when you disagree with someone, or when you have an issue to address, but make sure to do so as soon as possible. Don't let it fester.

3. Seek first to understand. As challenging as it can be, the best approach in any conflict situation is to listen with as much understanding and empathy as possible—even when we're feeling angry or defensive. If we can understand where the other person or people are coming from, even if we don't agree, we have a good chance of being able to work things out.

4. Use "I" statements. If someone does or says something and we have a specific reaction to it, that's real. If we judge someone, make a generalization about them, or accuse them of something, not only is it factually untrue (it's just our opinion), it most likely will trigger a defensive response (because we're usually being self-righteous in that scenario). We must own our opinions as ours, not speak them like they're the truth. Using "I" statements allows us to speak from a place of authenticity and ownership, ideally without blame or judgment. There's a big difference when we say "I'm feeling frustrated" versus "You are frustrating."

5. Go for a win-win. The only real way to have a conflict resolved authentically is when it's a true win-win for everyone involved. This doesn't necessarily mean that each person gets his or her way. It does, however, mean that everyone gets heard, honored, and listened to. And, when and if possible—we make compromises that leave everyone empowered and in partnership.

6. Acknowledge others. Whether it's a one-on-one conversation, a situation that involves a few people, or a discussion that includes the whole team, acknowledgment is essential to resolving conflict effectively. Thank the other people involved in the conflict for being willing and able to engage. Thank them for their courage and their truth. Acknowledgment isn't about agreement; it's about honoring and appreciating the *willingness* to have a tough conversation, which is brave all the way around.

7. Get support and have compassion. Conflicts often bring up fear and cut to the core of our most vulnerable insecurities. Therefore, it's critical to reach out for authentic support (not necessarily agreement on the topic) from those who can help us work through the issue and resolve it in a healthy and responsible way. It's also important to have compassion with ourselves and others as we attempt to engage in these conversations. Usually they aren't fun or easy, but they are necessary for us personally, for our relationships, and for the success of the team.

Feedback

One of the most important sweaty-palmed conversations for us to have in our teams involves giving and receiving feedback. And while feedback is usually built into the manager-employee relationship, great teams have the ability to give and receive feedback with their peers, back and forth with their manager, and all the way around. Furthermore, it's important to remember that feedback can be especially tricky and sensitive for most of us.

I heard another great interview on Marc Maron's *WTF* podcast with Bradley Whitford. Bradley's an actor who has appeared on Broadway, TV, and in films for the past 35 years. He played the role of Josh Lyman on one of my favorite TV shows of all time, *The West Wing*. In his conversation with Marc, Bradley talked about his reaction to getting feedback from directors. He said, "If I'm honest, anytime a director has ever said anything to me, I go through three silent beats (in my head).

Fuck you.
I suck.
Okay, what?

And, I really believe that is a universal response."

When I heard him say this, I laughed out loud. I'm not an actor, but I could totally relate to this reaction, especially when getting feedback on stuff that really matters to me—like my writing, speaking, parenting, body, finances, marriage, health, or business.

As leaders, team members, and human beings, we have to remember that just about everyone who receives feedback will experience those three internal beats. And, if we want our feedback to land well, or if we want to be able to take in what's being said to us in a way that's helpful, we need to do everything we can to get to *Okay, what?*, which is where the real growth can occur. If the people around us, or we ourselves, get stuck in that first beat, *Fuck you*, the defensiveness won't allow the wisdom and value of the feedback to take hold, and it can also damage the relationship in the process. If we or anyone else gets stuck in the second beat of *I suck*, we end up feeling self-critical, bad about ourselves, inferior, or disempowered, which doesn't allow the feedback to be valuable. This can also negatively impact our self-esteem, and can additionally leave us feeling resentful or self-protective.

Even though giving and receiving feedback can be challenging for most of us, it's necessary and important for our individual and collective success. Based on its extensive study of organizational performance worldwide, Officevibe reports that turnover rates are 14.9 percent lower in companies that implement regular employee feedback programs, 4 out of 10 people are actively disengaged when they get little or no feedback, and 65 percent of employees want more feedback.

Growth Mindset

One of the best things we can do to move beyond defensiveness and self-criticism when receiving feedback is to embrace a growth mindset. As I wrote about extensively in *Bring Your Whole Self to Work*, the concept of growth mindset was initially developed by Stanford professor and research psychologist Carol Dweck. According to her decades of research on learning, achievement, and success, we all have a mindset—a perception we hold about ourselves. Our mindset has a significant effect on our ability to learn and acquire new skills, as well as on our personal relationships, our professional success, our ability to navigate change, our resilience, and many other important aspects of work and life. The fundamental distinction that Dweck developed is what she calls the difference between a "fixed" and a "growth" mindset.

With a **fixed mindset**, we believe our basic qualities, like our talent or intelligence, are fixed traits. We spend our time documenting our intelligence or talent, instead of developing it. We also believe that talent alone creates success—without effort. With a **growth mindset**, we believe that our most basic abilities can be developed through dedication and hard work, that brains and talent are just a starting point. This view creates a love of learning, a desire for constant feedback, and a necessary resilience—all of which are essential for great accomplishment.

By adopting a growth mindset personally, and creating a culture on our team that is focused on learning, growth, and development, we look at everything that comes our way, including and especially feedback, as an opportunity to improve and evolve. Knowing that the feedback we get from team members is meant to help us, and remembering that if we utilize it we might improve, we can avoid getting stuck in a place of defensiveness or self-criticism. Reminding ourselves that the person giving us feedback isn't trying to make us feel bad or attack us, allows us to have compassion for ourselves when we do feel defensive or self-critical, which can help us shift into a growth mindset and more quickly get to *Okay, what?*

An effective way to enhance our ability to receive feedback is to ask for it proactively—which also happens to be a great way to practice embracing a growth mindset. Receiving feedback is essential to our development and success. And the more willing we are to seek it out and take it in, the more of it we'll get and the better we'll become at incorporating it. Doing this also models important growth mindset behavior for those around us and creates both the giving and receiving of feedback as a cultural norm within our team and organization. And, when we ask for feedback, we're much less likely to get defensive or to be self-critical when we receive it.

In February 2019, I was on the phone with some members of the HR team from Fidelity Investments. We were talking about the importance of feedback and how to create a feedback culture. At one point in the conversation, Andrea Hough, head of talent, said to me, "How would you feel if I said, 'Hey Mike, I have some feedback for you'?"

Even though she was asking this hypothetically, I felt myself stiffen up a bit and get nervous in that moment. She paused and said, "Notice how that question makes you feel. Now, what if I asked you, 'Hey Mike, do you have any feedback for me?' That's a totally different conversation, right?"

Again, even in the hypothetical, I had a much different reaction. If we ask for feedback from others, we go into that conversation ready, willing, and open to receive it. And when we give others permission to give us feedback, it's usually much easier and less stressful for them to do so.

According to a study conducted by psychologist Tessa West of NYU for the NeuroLeadership Institute, asking for feedback is also beneficial from a neuroscience perspective, as it helps reduce the automatic fight-or-flight threat response in our nervous system that often occurs in feedback discussions. When we ask for feedback proactively, we tend to create more psychological safety for ourselves and others than exists in a giver-led approach. This safety is crucial during these sweaty-palmed conversations because our brains will be in a much better state for performing complex cognitive functions and for taking in the feedback in a positive, productive, and growth mindset way.

Giving Feedback Effectively

As challenging and vulnerable as receiving feedback can be, giving it can also be quite difficult. According to the same NYU study, we don't just have that automatic fight-or-flight threat response in our nervous system when we're receiving feedback, we also have it when we're giving it. So it's essential to have some compassion for ourselves when we're in situations where we have to give feedback to others. And it's also important that we enhance our capacity—emotionally and practically—for giving feedback.

In addition to all we've talked about in this chapter thus far, there are four key things to remember when giving feedback to others. Keeping them in mind can help us get past their defensiveness and self-criticism so that our feedback can be well-received and have the positive impact we're intending.

1. Intention. It's critical to check in with ourselves about the intention behind our feedback. In other words, why are we giving it in the first place? Do we genuinely want the other person to be more successful? Are we annoyed with this person and want to let them know why? Do we have any conscious or unconscious bias? Are we trying to prove something or defend ourselves? Do we want to control them or the situation?

There are all kinds of reasons why we give feedback to others, and sometimes there is more than one. But being real with ourselves about our motivation can help us determine whether it's even going to be helpful. Assuming we decide that it is, making sure our intention is genuine and positive will make it more likely that the person will be receptive to it. And by giving feedback to others on our team with positive intention, we set the tone for our culture in this regard.

2. Permission. Unsolicited feedback, even if it's spot on and valuable, can be hard to take and even disrespectful. Asking someone if they're open to our feedback, while sometimes stressful, is important to do and much better than just launching into it. This is true even if we're their boss, parent, or mentor, or in any other type of relationship where permission for our feedback may seem implied. Making sure that we have explicit permission to give feedback shows that we respect and value the person to whom we're giving it. It also usually makes feedback feel less like judgment and more like help, allowing the person to be more receptive to what we have to say. Creating a team standard that we have permission to give each other feedback is also important. And, even if we do that, asking someone for specific permission in the moment before giving it is essential.

3. Skill. Giving feedback effectively takes skill. And even though it can be challenging, it's definitely something we can improve upon the more we practice and dedicate ourselves to doing it. Because giving and receiving feedback can be a vulnerable experience for everyone involved, it requires attention, commitment, awareness, and courage to do it well. It's often the hardest type of sweaty-palmed conversation. The more willing we are to do it, the more we can develop our skill of giving feedback successfully. And there are, of course, different ways to give feedback effectively. Oftentimes, we may give it directly and explicitly as part of a review, development conversation, or team debrief. Other times it may be subtler and not even seem like feedback at all, but more of a question, suggestion, or conversation.

4. Relationship. The most important aspect of giving effective feedback is the relationship we have with the person or people we're giving it to. We can have the most positive intention, explicit permission, and a lot of skill in how we deliver it—but if our relationship isn't strong or it's actively strained, it'll be very difficult for us to give feedback to someone and have them receive it well. I could get the same exact feedback from two different people but react to it quite differently depending on my relationship with each of them. Let's say, in one case, I know the person cares about me, appreciates me, and believes in me. I'm much more likely to be open to their feedback and to take it positively. Therefore, making sure the relationships we have are strong and authentic helps us ensure that we can give feedback effectively when we need to do so. If the person giving feedback is someone I don't know as well or may have some unresolved issues with, it's less likely that I'll be open and take their feedback well. If we find ourselves in a situation where we have to give feedback to someone with whom we don't have a strong relationship, it's important to know that this will definitely have an impact. Anything we can do to acknowledge this in an authentic way and work to enhance or improve the relationship will benefit our ability to provide feedback to them in the present moment and in the future.

All four of these things—intention, permission, skill, and relationship—are important to remember when giving feedback. And they're also important to think about from a growth mindset perspective when receiving feedback. We want to be sure to check in with and pay attention to what the other person's intention might be with their feedback for us, to explicitly grant others permission to give us feedback, to communicate about how we like feedback to be given, and to proactively work to strengthen our relationships with the people around us.

Giving and receiving feedback isn't easy, but it's so important for our growth and development, as well as that of our team. Being able to embrace and even enjoy the sweaty-palmed nature of feedback is something that can allow us and our team to perform our absolute best.

Radical Candor

As we're thinking about and talking about embracing sweaty-palmed conversations, and specifically about giving feedback to those on our team, an important concept to understand is "radical candor." My friend Kim Scott has been a guest on my podcast twice. She created an important framework and wrote a best-selling book called *Radical Candor*. According to Kim, "Radical candor is caring personally while challenging directly. It's guidance that's kind and clear, specific and sincere." Based on this framework, if we care personally but aren't willing or able to challenge directly, it's what Kim calls "ruinous empathy." If we challenge directly but don't care personally, that's "obnoxious aggression." And if we don't care or challenge at all, it then becomes "manipulative insincerity."

I love this idea of radical candor and there's a reason why so many leaders, teams, and organizations have adopted this language and framework. It's a way to understand, think about, and act upon having those important sweaty-palmed conversations—one-on-one, in a group, with our team, across our organization, and even with those whom we interact externally, both professionally and personally.

I heard Jeff Weiner, CEO of LinkedIn, speak about the importance of giving feedback to a manager (and receiving feedback as a leader) at a Wisdom 2.0 conference a few years ago. Jeff said, "A lot of people are concerned about giving their manager constructive feedback—worried about them taking it the wrong way and becoming punitive. First things first, if you're working for someone who would be punitive because you're providing them constructive feedback, you need to think long and hard about whether or not that's the right person for you to be working for. Now granted, some people aren't in a position where they have a choice. They have to put food on the table. But if you're fortunate enough where you do have choices, you want to be open, honest, and constructive in those situations. . . . It's a gift when people on my team come to me and say, 'You know, I thought you did this well, and I think you could do this better.'"

🧩 Start, Stop, Continue 🧩

One of my favorite ways for both eliciting and giving radically candid feedback safely and productively is the Start, Stop, Continue technique, which I introduced in *Bring Your Whole Self to Work*. I've used different versions of this process with people, leaders, and entire teams for a number of years and have seen remarkable results.

Here's how it works: When you meet with someone one-on-one, whether it's your manager, a peer, a cross-functional partner, a direct report, or anyone else, you can ask for feedback in this specific way.

Start: "What can I *start* doing that I'm currently not doing that you think will make me more effective in my role and in working with you?"

Stop: "What can I *stop* doing that I'm currently doing that you think may be getting in my way of being as successful as I can be and as easy as possible for you to work with?"

Continue: "And, what do you suggest that I *continue* doing that is allowing me to be effective in my work and helpful in my partnership with you?"

It's important to set some context for the other person before asking them these questions and to let them know you really want them to be honest with you in their responses. These questions tend to make it fairly easy for the other person to think about, answer, and give you real feedback, but it's important to let them know specifically that you want them to be authentic and that there won't be any retribution for doing so.

You can also request that they ask you these three questions in response, which will give you the opportunity to give them feedback in the same way. This process is something that can be done on a regular basis in one-on-one meetings so that there is constant feedback flowing back and forth. It's also a very specific way to make the sweaty-palmed nature of feedback a bit easier and more accessible.

Lots of people I've taught this technique to over the years have implemented versions of Start, Stop, Continue with their own managers, direct reports, and fellow team members. I use it myself to influence and inspire action and growth with some of the teams I work with in two different ways.

One fairly simple way is as a brainstorming and action-inspiring exercise at the end of a team session, offsite, or retreat. Whether we've spent a half day, a full day, or a number of days together, I often invite the team to spend some time reflecting on what they can *start, stop,* and *continue* doing as a team to enhance their teamwork, connection, culture, and overall performance. I usually have them break up into smaller groups of four or five people, and each group brainstorms things in all three categories. We then have a full-group discussion and write down the best ideas in each category on flip charts or whiteboards. These lists are then typed up and sent out to the entire team, and someone or a small group of people usually takes on the responsibility for implementing the key changes and holding the team accountable for them.

The second way I use the Start, Stop, Continue technique is for individual feedback in a group setting. This one takes quite a bit of skill, maturity, and emotional intelligence from everyone involved, but it can be incredibly powerful and can take the growth of your team to a whole new level. In this case, it's best to do with a small, intact team of 10 people or fewer.

For this particular process to work, however, there has to be some real trust and psychological safety established—with the team in general and also specifically in the moment as we do the exercise. This is crucial, and is one of my most important roles when I work with teams like this. In some cases, we may have already done an exercise like "If you really knew me . . . " as a group, so that can help create a deeper level of connection and safety. But regardless of what has come before, I ask the group if they're willing to do a risky but valuable exercise, and if they'd like to get some helpful, authentic feedback from their fellow team members. Even if they seem a little scared, which most people are, I make sure to check in with the group before we move forward. I also let them know that nothing anyone is going to say is the "truth," it's just their opinion (as most feedback is, by the way). I also ask if they want their teammates to just be "nice," or if they want genuine feedback with the intention of helping them be the best they can be. Almost everyone says they want it to be real.

I also remind them that the purpose of the exercise is for everyone to learn and grow personally, and for them to grow as a team. For the individuals and the team to get the most out of the exercise, they must consciously embrace a growth mindset—which is all about being open to learning and growing, even if it might be uncomfortable.

Once I've set all this up and have gotten permission and buy-in from the members of the team, we start with the first person, usually the leader. I often check in with him or her before the session to ask if they're up to doing this exercise and willing to go first, and if they think their team is mature enough and in a good enough place in terms of morale, trust, connection, and collective mental-emotional state to do it. The more openly the leader is willing to take feedback from their team (in other words, to model growth mindset and embrace sweaty-palmed conversations in real time), the easier and safer it will be for the rest of the team to do so.

People then start to offer things to their leader that they can *start*, *stop*, or *continue* doing. After that, we go through the entire group and give each person a chance to be on the "feedback seat." The person receiving feedback is asked to just listen and write down what they hear, not discuss the feedback or defend themselves in any way. They are welcome to ask questions if they want some specific clarification.

Most teams I've done this with have found it incredibly valuable—both in terms of the feedback they're able to receive and give specifically, and in terms of the collective bonding and growth it encourages. When we debrief after the exercise, people are often amazed that it wasn't as difficult or painful as they expected, and that despite their fears they actually found it refreshing and helpful in a practical way.

Feedback is such an important instigator of growth. And one of the ways to enhance our skills, increase our performance, and strengthen our culture, is by soliciting and valuing the feedback of our teammates. Doing this is courageous, vulnerable, and essential. The more willing we are to embrace the sweaty-palmed conversations involved in giving and receiving feedback, the better we can perform as individuals and as a team.

The Leader's Role in Embracing Sweaty-Palmed Conversations

Leaders play an important role in encouraging, modeling, and making it safe and conducive for sweaty-palmed conversations to take place within the team in a healthy and productive way. Whether you have a specific leadership position or you just want to influence others around you as a leader, here are a few specific things you can do and think about in this regard:

Embrace conflict. A frequent complaint I hear from teams I work with is that their leader doesn't like conflict and tends to shut it down when it arises. This is one of the worst things we can do as leaders—it stifles debate, discussion, innovation, ideas, creativity, and so much more. Even though it might be tricky, scary, and uncomfortable, the more willing we are as leaders to embrace and even encourage healthy conflict, the more open the team can be and the better the solutions and outcomes will be. It's critical to remember that conflict is essential for growth, trust, and collaboration. The more willing we are to remind ourselves and each other of this, and to take actions that are conducive to making conflict as open and productive as possible, the better off we will be personally as leaders and the stronger the team will be in the process.

Talk about the elephant in the room. There are often sensitive issues, uncomfortable topics, and difficult situations that arise. And while it's important for us as leaders to use discretion, to honor confidentiality, and to be able to keep certain information private when necessary, one of the most important things we can do is to talk about touchy subjects directly—sooner rather than later. As the saying goes, "Bad news doesn't age well." Most of the time, some or all of the team members are aware of the issue, and although it might be uncomfortable, avoiding it usually makes things worse. Not only is it liberating to talk about the elephant in the room, when we do so, we can at the very least relieve some tension. More likely we'll also have the possibility of using the collective wisdom of the group to address the challenge directly and come up with potential solutions. Additionally, we model courage, vulnerability, and growth mindset when we do this, which is beneficial to the situation and to the culture of the team.

Don't triangulate or gossip. Part of our job as leaders is to listen to our team members when they come to us with issues or challenges, including when those things are specifically about other members of the team or the company. While we want to do everything we can to make it safe for people to open up with us and tell us how they're truly feeling, we also want to make sure not to triangulate or gossip. Triangulation is when someone comes to us with feedback for another person, but wants us to deliver it instead of them doing so directly. Gossip is, of course, simply talking negatively about others behind their backs. Doing either of these things damages trust and psychological safety. If someone comes to us complaining about a co-worker, and in our attempt to empathize we jump in and start gossiping about the person they're talking about, it might make them feel good initially that we agreed with their assessment, but ultimately it will leave them feeling nervous and insecure that we may be gossiping about *them* behind closed doors.

And, when we triangulate and don't encourage our teams to have direct, open conversations with each other, not only are we less likely to help them resolve issues, we model behavior that is the *opposite* of embracing sweaty-palmed conversations, which sets up further negativity and unhealthiness for the team. We want to challenge the people on our team to have these tough and important conversations with each other or at least be willing to help facilitate these discussions so that things get dealt with and resolved.

Ask for and take in feedback. Creating a feedback culture and having a team that embraces a growth mindset allows everyone to develop, perform, and thrive. The best way to inspire this is to model the behavior ourselves. Proactively asking for feedback from the people who report to us, as well as from our peers, our manager, and others, is a great way to ensure that we're constantly growing and changing, and also to show our team members what it looks like, thus making it safer and easier for them to follow suit. Using the Start, Stop, Continue technique in one-on-one meetings is a great way to practice this. And, as important as *asking* for feedback is, people are going to be paying attention to what we *do* with their feedback. So, the more willing we are to thank them for it, act on it, and share our own growth process with the team, the more encouraged they'll be to give us additional feedback and the more they'll trust our authenticity in wanting it and using it.

Have regular check-ins and constant development conversations. The days of the annual performance reviews seem to be over in many of the most progressive organizations. The pace of business and the nature of how we work and communicate has forced us to change the way we think about managing people and performance, developing talent, and coaching. The best leaders I work with are constantly checking in with the people on their team and having development conversations all the time. While they may happen during formal one-on-one meetings or even in specific ways quarterly, biannually, or annually, it's important to think of your role as being an ongoing coach for all the people on your team. Your ability to give on-the-spot, real-time feedback is often what can have the most significant impact. Finding creative and effective ways to have consistent check-ins and regular development conversations with everyone around you will benefit you, them, and the team.

The Team Member's Role in Embracing Sweaty-Palmed Conversations

Each person on the team plays a vital role in making it safe and conducive for healthy conflict, productive feedback, and any other type of sweaty-palmed conversations to take place. This is not just up to the leader of our team or the senior leaders in the organization, although they do play important roles. Each of the suggestions listed previously about what leaders can do may also apply to us as team members. And there are some additional things to think about and do as a member of the team that can positively influence our ability as individuals and as a group to embrace sweaty-palmed conversations.

Speak up. We talked about the importance of speaking up in the previous pillar with respect to diversity, inclusion, and belonging. In addition to having the courage to address those important topics, there are often issues, disagreements, things we find confusing, or stuff that happens more broadly that we end up gossiping or complaining about to our peers, friends, or others. Instead of sitting on these things, not saying something in the moment, or talking about them after the fact or to those who feel "safe" for various reasons, it's important that we challenge ourselves to speak up. This may mean we bring it up in the moment, in the meeting, or with the entire group. It may also mean that we approach our manager, a peer, or someone else after the fact and address the issue directly. Having the courage to speak up, even and especially when we're scared, is essential to our growth, as well as to the culture and success of our team.

If you have a complaint, make sure you express it proactively. There are two types of complaints: idle complaints and proactive complaints. Idle complaints— whining to others about things we don't like and commiserating about stuff that bugs us about other people, the team, or the company—are often harmful and make it harder for conflicts to get resolved in a healthy way. They create negativity, separation, gossip, and disempowerment. However, similar to speaking up, proactive complaints are when we have an issue and we're willing to bring it up directly to someone or a group of people who can potentially *do* something about it. We may or may not get our way, but if we're willing to own it and talk about it directly, we might be able to get an issue resolved or encourage a necessary change. Even if nothing changes, at the very least we know we did something proactively to try to make things better and we don't waste our time and energy complaining to others in a way that won't help, and actually might make things worse.

Give feedback to your manager, peers, and others. Even though it can be risky and often doesn't seem like it's necessarily part of our job, giving feedback to our manager, our peers, and others with whom we work is an important part of our collective success, growth, and performance. It takes courage to have these types of sweaty-palmed conversations, but it can not only have a positive impact on those we give the feedback to, it will also enhance our collective capacity and the culture of growth for our team. Remember the four things we discussed in this chapter that can allow our feedback to be received in the most positive and productive way possible: intention, permission, skill, and relationship. Knowing that most people will initially

115

react with defensiveness and/or self-criticism, it's key that we use our emotional intelligence and act with courage and compassion for ourselves and others in this process. Seeing if they're open to using the Start, Stop, Continue technique can be a good way to engage in these feedback discussions specifically.

Make sure you're getting the feedback you want and need. Although most of us do get some feedback from our managers and others, many of us aren't getting as much of the kind of feedback we most want and need to be as successful as we can be. Don't waste time and energy blaming your manager or anyone else. Instead, ask for the specific feedback you want, both in terms of the cadence and the content. This is about owning your career and your development. You and your manager, as well as everyone else on the team, have to work together to make sure growth and development is happening. Even the best managers have blind spots and aren't usually going to pay as much attention to us as we'd like. The catch-22 is that while we may wish we were getting more or different feedback, it can also be uncomfortable and vulnerable, so it doesn't always feel good, even if there's a lot of trust with our manager and psychological safety on our team. The more overt we are about asking for feedback and the more specific we are about when, how, and what will work best for us, the more likely we are to get what we need. And by modeling this for our team members and others, we encourage those around us to do the same and make it easier to have these types of sweaty-palmed conversations.

Take feedback as a gift. As Jeff Weiner said, feedback is a gift. When someone cares about us enough, has the courage to speak up, and is willing to be vulnerable to have a sweaty-palmed feedback conversation with us, the best thing we can do is to take in what they're saying as an offering. It doesn't mean we have to agree with them or necessarily act on it specifically, but the more willing we are to consider their feedback as a gift being presented to us, the more likely we are to allow it to impact us positively. Having compassion for ourselves if we either get defensive or go into that place of self-criticism, which most of us do initially, we can quickly shift into a growth mindset approach and look for the gold in what's being said. Plus, the better we are at taking feedback from others, the safer we'll make it for people to give to us, and the more helpful feedback we'll receive.

What Your Team Can Do to Embrace Sweaty-Palmed Conversations

As a team there are some specific things to think about, talk about, and do to make it easier to embrace sweaty-palmed conversations in a productive way. Here are some ideas:

Think and talk about conflict. One of the ways to make embracing conflict in a healthy way easier is to have some real awareness of ourselves and our team members with respect to conflict. How do we feel and act when we're in conflict? How do others feel and act when they're in conflict? Does this change when the conflict is one-on-one versus in a group setting or among the entire team? These and other questions like them are good to think about and discuss directly and openly with the people we work with. The more open and aware we are about our own relationship to conflict and how we react when a conflict arises, as well as that for those around us, the better understanding we'll have and the more effective we can be in those sweaty-palmed conversations with each other and as a team.

Conflict is an important part of life, relationships, and teamwork. Talking about it more can benefit us and those around us in many ways. Being able to embrace conflict and utilize it productively means understanding how we and others around us relate and react to it, which is why it's so important for us to think and talk about it as a team.

Have the tough conversation in the room, not the easy one after the meeting. Among the most destructive dynamics I see with teams are the side conversations that happen outside of team meetings. The "meeting after the meeting" can often be damaging to the trust, psychological safety, and culture of the team. The more willing we are to have the important conversations that need to take place in the room with everyone, not after the fact with just a select group of people who we think already agree with us, the better off we'll be as a team. As Dan Henkle talked about with his team at Old Navy, if we make a commitment to be "divided together, but united apart" we set ourselves up for success. Being willing to engage in sweaty-palmed conversations with each other as a group and making a commitment to not gossip about each other or throw one another under the bus, creates an environment where we know that we have each other's backs. And the more we do this, the better we'll get, the safer it'll become, and the more we'll model it for others in our organization.

Remember that alignment doesn't mean agreement. Building on the theme of "divided together, united apart," an important distinction that great teams understand is the difference between agreement and alignment. Agreement is when we all come to the same conclusion and see things exactly the same way. It can be wonderful when this happens, but it isn't all that common, and in most cases, isn't necessary. As we discussed in the previous chapter, a team that has members with different backgrounds, as well as skill sets, personalities, and styles, is ideal for optimal performance. When we have a diverse team and we also have smart, talented, passionate, opinionated people, we're not going to agree on everything. Debate and conflict are important and healthy, as we've been discussing throughout this chapter. So if our goal is to get to a place where we all agree before we move forward on decisions or take actions, we slow ourselves down and set ourselves up for failure. What we want to do is focus on *alignment*. This means we make a commitment to having authentic discussions and debates about important topics and issues so that everyone gets to speak up, weigh in, and share their views. Once we've gone through that process and come to a decision, we align ourselves and commit to it. We do this in service of the team, the larger goals, and the organization.

Make sure everyone's voice is heard. Most teams have certain people—based on their roles or personalities—who take up more space, speak more often, or have more influence on the dynamic of the team and the decisions that get made. This is fairly natural and normal for teams, and doesn't, in and of itself, make the team ineffective or dysfunctional. It's important, however, for every member of the team and the team as a whole to be aware of these dynamics and to be able to call them out if and when they become problematic.

When it comes to engaging in healthy conflict, giving and receiving feedback as a team, and addressing other various sweaty-palmed conversations, make sure that everyone on the team is given a chance to have their voice heard. This doesn't mean that each member has to weigh in on every single issue. However, it does mean that when it comes to really important discussions, topics, and decisions, the team is mindful of some of the personality, role, and communication dynamics of the team, and specifically gives those who may not always speak up as much as others the time, space, and permission to voice their perspective.

Give and receive feedback as a team. Teams that create a culture where feedback happens in real time and with one another as a group have a distinct advantage. Sometimes this might mean that we take time to reflect on the overall performance and culture of the team as a whole. It might involve the team members giving their leader specific feedback. And it might mean that various members of the team have the courage to give feedback to other members. If all of this is done with a growth mindset approach, and the intention behind the feedback is to allow every individual and the team collectively to perform at their absolute best, this can be incredibly powerful and productive. Once again, using the Start, Stop, Continue technique—for the group as a whole or for individuals on the team—can be incredibly effective.

Embracing sweaty-palmed conversations isn't always fun or easy. Whether it's talking about a sensitive topic, engaging in a challenging debate, or exchanging radically candid feedback, these tough conversations are foundational to our success and they're necessary for us to create a team culture of high performance, trust, and belonging.

PILLAR #4

....

CARE ABOUT AND
CHALLENGE EACH OTHER

....

Jason Hughes is the chairman, CEO, and co-owner of Hughes Marino, a commercial real estate company based in San Diego with additional offices in Los Angeles, Orange County, San Francisco, Seattle, and New York. I've had a chance to partner with Jason, his wife, president, COO, and fellow co-owner, Shay, and the team at Hughes Marino over the past nine years as they've grown their company and their culture in remarkable ways. Among the many awards Hughes Marino has received, it was named the #1 Best Workplace in the Nation in 2018 in the Small and Medium Business category by *Fortune* magazine.

One of the things that Jason, Shay, and their team do as well as almost any company I've ever worked with is that they challenge each other to be the absolute best they can be. And they do it with a foundation of genuine care for one another. They balance having an incredibly high standard of excellence while also making sure everyone is nurtured and supported.

When I asked Jason about this, he said, "I feel so incredibly vested in everyone's happiness and success that I literally wake up in the middle of the night thinking about it. I think to myself, *Have I connected with this person lately? How's he doing? How's she feeling? What can I do to give them some love and support? What can I do to help lift them higher in their career? How can I help build their confidence? Where do they need some extra attention?* "

Jason went on to say, "I literally think about these types of questions for our teammates all the time. It reminds me a bit about of how we raised our children. I love them so much—and I want to give them anything I can to help them be successful. While I love my team a bit differently than I love our kids, of course, I tend to have a lot of the same feelings and concerns about them, and want to do whatever I can to take care of them, and to push them to be their best.

"The people on our team are capable of so much more than they realize, and I just want to help them break down any mental barriers to accomplish and experience all that they can. It has been so fulfilling to see our team members grow as individuals—both professionally and personally. It's truly the highlight of my career to witness their success."

The team at Hughes Marino has built an incredibly strong and successful culture where they bring out the best in one another, because they know they're cared about deeply and at the same time they have healthy high standards by which they expect themselves and each other to perform.

I've been a part of lots of teams, in sports and business, and over the past 20 years I've had a chance to work with so many high-performing teams, like the one at Hughes Marino. Through all of my experience and research, I've found that two conditions most effectively enable a team to create a culture of high performance, trust, and belonging:

1. Caring About Each Other. Caring about the people on our team is about making sure they are nurtured and valued—not just for what they *do*, but for who they *are*. It also has to do with it being safe for us to make mistakes, ask for help, speak up, be ourselves, and disagree. In other words, as we've discussed in the previous chapters, this is about feeling psychologically safe, knowing we're included and that we belong, and having the confidence to have sweaty-palmed conversations. Caring environments are also filled with a genuine sense of kindness, compassion, and appreciation, where people are seen and supported as human beings.

2. Challenging Each Other. Challenging each other is about having high expectations, which are essential for people and teams to thrive. But these expectations have to be healthy—meaning there is a high standard of excellence, not an insatiable, unhealthy pressure to be perfect. We almost always get what we expect from others; however, if we expect perfection, everyone falls short and people aren't set up to succeed. Healthy high expectations are about setting a high bar and challenging everyone (our teammates and ourselves) to be the absolute best we can be. This also has to do with being clear about our standards and goals, holding each other accountable, fully committing ourselves to the team, and demanding excellence from one another in a healthy and empowering way.

We often think that in order to have a high bar and push each other we can't also be caring. Or we think that if we care about and nurture one another, we can't also expect a lot from our teammates. Actually, the goal for us as team members, leaders, and teams as a whole is to be able do both at the same time. It's not one of these things at the expense of the other, it's being able to do them simultaneously and passionately. Creating an environment that supports both caring about and challenging each other takes courage on everyone's part, and at times goes against conventional wisdom. But being willing to focus on both of these things, and encouraging others to do the same, creates the conditions for everyone to succeed at the highest level.

This combination of caring about and challenging each other is the secret sauce of high-performing teams. And while this is fairly easy to understand as a concept, it's not quite as easy to practice in reality. As we have done with each of the previous pillars in this book, let's address some of the things that can make this one difficult so that we can then talk about what it will take for you and your team to genuinely care about each other and passionately challenge one another in the most effective way possible.

Hard to Balance. Most of us are stronger in one of these things than the other. We may be good at caring about and nurturing others, but find it more difficult to challenge and expect a lot from the people on our team in a productive way. Or, we may be hard-driving, focused, and more than willing to push people but find it more difficult to genuinely express our care and appreciation for them. Oftentimes, when we become aware of this imbalance, there's a tendency to lessen or lower the one we feel is strong in order to balance them out. In reality, the best thing we can do is to challenge ourselves to raise our capacity for the one of these two things that we find more difficult. This, by its nature, isn't all that easy to do. The ability to both expect a lot from others and care about them—and finding the right balance of these two things—is challenging for most of us, and it's a dynamic process that is continuously evolving.

Constant Change. Heraclitus, a Greek philosopher, said, "Change is the only constant in life." He was right, and this statement is as true as ever in today's modern business world. Things are changing all the time. The pace and intensity of change presents a number of potential challenges, especially with respect to our teams. Caring about and challenging each other is based on our ability to build strong and lasting relationships. And when people are moving in and out of the team, when what we do and how we do it constantly evolves, and when the people we report to and interact with change, it can be difficult. All of these things make it more challenging to build strong connections and feel the sense of safety and belonging necessary for us to really commit to one another and to the team in the way we truly need to in order for us to succeed.

Fear. Fear gets in our way in so many aspects of work and life. Related to teamwork and collaboration, and specifically the ability to expect a lot and nurture the people on our team, there seem to be two main fears we have. First, we worry that if we truly care about people we might get hurt, disappointed, or taken advantage of. These things are painful and most of us have experienced them before in various ways. Our fear of getting hurt has us hold back and protect ourselves. Second, we fear that if we push people, challenge our teammates, and hold them accountable for being their absolute best, they might do the same for us, and therefore we might fail, disappoint them, or be put into difficult situations. Even though most of us want to be pushed in a way that brings out the best in us, it can be scary. Therefore, we often make an unspoken agreement with the people around us, *I won't push you too hard if you don't push me too hard. This way we can play it safe, not get hurt, and not embarrass ourselves.*

Being "Nice." Most of us were taught to be "nice." When we were growing up, we were told to be "good boys" and "good girls" by our parents, teachers, and others. And as we move through our lives and careers, being nice continues to be encouraged and reinforced in many ways. However, sometimes our desire to be nice gets in the way of our doing and saying what's needed to succeed. In other words, our concern about upsetting people holds us back from the sweaty-palmed conversations that might make the biggest difference for them, us, and our team. We don't speak up, call something out, challenge someone, or hold people accountable because we can't figure out how to do it or say it in a nice way. Being kind and caring toward others, which is essential for healthy relationships and strong teams, isn't about being nice. Niceness is often about us wanting people to like us or acting in ways we think are acceptable and appropriate, even if we're being phony or inauthentic. Pushing our teammates and challenging them to be their best may not always be the nicest thing to do, but it's often essential for their success and that of our team. Being nice often gets in our way of being great— individually and collectively.

Lack of Incentive. As we talked about in the Introduction, there are a number of things that make teamwork challenging; we weren't trained to work in teams, we get caught in the "Us versus Them" trap, and we focus so much on ourselves. All of these things, and others, can sometimes make it confusing and challenging to see the incentive of really committing to our team. It's not like we get a group paycheck or a group promotion, right? We're most often evaluated and rewarded individually. And, because many of the specific deadlines and deliverables we have to manage are focused on our personal work and not the work of the entire team, it can take additional time, awareness, and even faith to see the direct link between our connection to our team and the success of what we're trying to accomplish ourselves. Depending on our specific role and the type of work we do, the practical incentive for us to work together with our team, and specifically to care about our teammates and challenge them passionately, may not be super clear. Whatever the case may be on this front, it takes real commitment and courage on our part to do this, which isn't always easy.

As with each of the previous chapters, addressing some of the things that make this particular pillar difficult isn't about whining or complaining, it's about acknowledging some of the things that can get in our way personally and collectively in this regard. By being aware of these challenges, we can make conscious choices to move beyond them and not let these things, and others, get in the way of our ability to care about and push our teammates in healthy and effective ways.

This fourth and final pillar builds on the three previous ones. We started with psychological safety, then talked about inclusion and belonging, then addressed the importance of sweaty-palmed conversations. Doing each of these things allows us the ability to talk about our team performing at the highest level, which is what this pillar is all about.

As we dive more deeply into specific ways you and your team can care about and challenge each other in a way that brings out the best in everyone, it's important for us to discuss a few specific mindsets and ideas that great teams understand and embody.

Being a Championship Team

As I wrote about in *Bring Your Whole Self to Work* and often speak about to groups, given my sports background I refer to teams who operate and perform at their peak level as "championship teams." There's an important difference between a *championship team* and a *team of champions*.

A championship team doesn't necessarily always win, but they play the game the right way, with passion, and with a commitment to one another as well as to the ultimate result. This type of team knows that it's greater than the sum of its parts. It's often chemistry and the below-the-line intangibles that we've been talking about throughout this book that separate the good teams from the great ones.

Teams of champions, on the other hand, might have great talent and motivated people, but they're often more focused on their own individual success. Championship teams know that talent is important, but they focus on the collective success of the team and the highest vision and goals of the group. As basketball legend Michael Jordan said, "Talent wins games, but teamwork and intelligence win championships."

With leadership teams specifically, I make this same distinction in a slightly different way: A team of champion leaders is a group of managers who focus on being the best they can be; and a championship leadership team is a group of leaders who realize that they're members of the same team, and that the more united and aligned they are, the more it benefits them, each other, and the people who report to them.

Additionally, there are two specific things that championship teams understand, from a mindset perspective, that allow them to come together and perform:

1. The difference between their role and their job. When most of us think about our "job," we think of what we do—engineering, sales, project management, marketing, human resources, legal, operations, design, finance, and so forth. While these descriptions may encapsulate what we do and the title we hold, they're not actually our job. If we're part of a team, we each have a functional role, of course, but our job is to help fulfill the goals, mission, and purpose of the team and company we belong to, whatever they may be. In other words, we're there to do whatever we can to *help the team win*. The challenge is that most of us take pride in our role and we want to do it really well, which is great. However, when we put our role (what we do specifically) over our job (helping the team win), things can get murky; our personal goals become more important to us than the goals of the team and organization. It takes commitment and courage, but groups and companies made up of people who understand this simple yet important distinction—who realize that everyone on the team has essentially the same job but different roles—have the ability to succeed at the highest level and with the most collaborative environment.

2. The difference between their first team and their second team. This concept is particularly important to managers at every level in an organization. If you're an individual contributor, your first (and only) team is usually pretty well defined. Most often it includes your peers—the people who report to the same manager as you. You may have a larger team that your intact team rolls up to, but since you don't really have a second team, your first team is fairly straightforward.

However, when I ask most managers to tell me about their team, they usually talk about their direct reports, or the larger organization that reports up to them if they happen to be a senior leader. This makes sense, especially when we get all the way up to the executive-team level within a company. Most leaders feel a sense of pride, ownership, and commitment to "their team"—since the people who report to them directly or roll up to them are the ones they're responsible for, are tasked with coaching and developing, and are evaluated themselves in large part based on how those people perform.

But leaders, leadership teams, and companies function best when they understand that their "first team" is actually the team they're a member of, and their "second team" is the team that reports to them. This may seem counterintuitive, because most leaders are going to spend a majority of their time focused on the team they manage. But for things to operate in the healthiest, most effective way, leadership teams should function as actual teams and support one another as peers and fellow members of the same team, not just as a group of managers who have the same boss. This can be tricky because things sometimes get competitive and priorities can be at odds with our peers, particularly at a senior leadership level. However, understanding that as leaders our peers are our first team and our reports are our second team, benefits everyone involved. And any misalignment on a leadership team (especially the higher up in the organization it occurs) creates exponential misalignment in the level or levels below.

Understanding these fundamental mindsets about teamwork gives us the framework to focus on some of the things we can do to enhance the performance and culture of our team, regardless of the specific role we play. Our ability to care about and challenge each other, and to remember that we're all in this together, has a lot to do with the environment around us and the performance of our team.

The Importance of Appreciation

I've been speaking about, writing about, and researching appreciation for the entire 20 years that I've been doing this work. I've touched on the power of appreciation in various ways in each of my previous four books, and I address it in almost every speech and seminar I deliver. In addition to being fascinated by this topic, I know from my research and experience that one of the most important traits of high-performing teams is that they appreciate each other.

In some cases, we know that appreciation can be an even more powerful and authentic motivator than money. Researchers from the London School of Economics found that financial incentives can actually backfire when it comes to motivating people. They did an analysis of 51 separate experiments and found overwhelming evidence that "incentives may reduce an employee's natural inclination to complete a task and derive pleasure from doing so." And, according to results of Glassdoor's

Employee Appreciation Survey, 53 percent of people said they would stay longer at their company if they felt more appreciated.

As we're talking specifically about caring for and challenging each other in this chapter, it's important to understand that appreciation is one of the best ways we can express our care for our teammates and others with whom we work. It also sets the foundation in our relationships and on our team that allows us to challenge each other in the most positive and effective way possible.

There is, however, an important distinction we must understand to fully utilize the power of appreciation with each other, our team, and anyone we interact with. It's the distinction between recognition and appreciation.

Recognition

Recognition is positive feedback based on results or performance. Sometimes recognition is given in a formal way—an award, a bonus, a promotion, a raise, an official announcement, a gift, or a public acknowledgment. Sometimes recognition is given more informally—a thank-you, a literal or figurative pat on the back, a note, or something simple letting us know we've done a good job. These things can be important, especially if they're done in a timely, generous, and genuine way. They're also often motivating and exciting.

Even if we get a little embarrassed, there are very few of us who don't like to be recognized for doing a good job. And getting a bonus, a raise, or an award is something that most of us enjoy very much.

But there are some limits to and issues with recognition. First, it's performance based—so it's conditional. Second, it's about the past, so it's based on what we've already done. Third, it's scarce. There's a limited amount of recognition to go around, and in some cases, it can be stressful when many people are vying for a finite amount of recognition. Finally, although many organizations have set up internal recognition programs that allow peers to recognize one another, the major forms of recognition (promotions, raises, bonuses, significant awards, etc.) usually have to come from above. This puts extra pressure on leaders and makes it more of a top-down exercise, not so much a team-oriented experience.

Appreciation

Appreciation, on the other hand, is about acknowledging a person's inherent value. It's not about recognizing their accomplishments or results; it's about appreciating who they are as a human being. In simple terms, recognition is about what we do; appreciation is about who we are. This is important for many reasons, but mainly because even when we have success, individually and collectively, there are often failures and challenges along the way. And even if there aren't, there may not be tangible results to recognize specifically or continuously. If we focus solely on positive outcomes, we miss out on lots of opportunities for connection, support, and appreciation. What most of us truly yearn for at work and in life is to be appreciated and cared about for who we are, not just what we do. And because appreciation is about recognizing people's value as human beings, not just rewarding them for their performance, it's not role or outcome specific. In other words, anyone can appreciate anyone else on the team, for any reason, and at any time. Focusing on and expressing appreciation for one another is a powerful way to demonstrate that we care about the people on our team. It's also necessary to our ability to challenge those around us in a healthy and productive way.

Think about the people in your life whom you've given either explicit or implicit permission to challenge you. You may not always love or agree with what they say or do, or how they do it, but you're willing to consider their feedback and you allow them to push you. Why? Because they're the smartest person you know or they have some special power? No, not usually. The people we allow to challenge us have personal credibility with us, and specifically, we know they appreciate us, value us, and care about us in an authentic way. This is one of the main reasons we listen to their feedback and we let them push us. Appreciation is the foundation to both caring about and challenging our teammates, and allowing them to care about and challenge us.

🧩 The Appreciation Seat Exercise 🧩

There are lots of ways—both big and small—for us to appreciate the people on our team. Some of these things can be done on a regular basis and others may happen at specific times, like team meetings, offsites, milestones, or other occasions. One of my favorite exercises to facilitate when I come in to work with a team at an offsite is what I call the Appreciation Seat.

This exercise, which I also talked about in *Bring Your Whole Self to Work*, is a great bonding experience; it specifically allows people on the team to express appreciation for one another and receive appreciation from their teammates, and it's an exemplification of caring about each other. I love this exercise and do it so often because it's fairly simple but has so much impact.

It's best to do it with your entire team if you can, though ideally with no more than 15 people, because of the time involved and also the intimate nature of this exercise. If the group is larger than 15, you can split the group up into smaller, sub-groups. Each person gets a turn in the Appreciation Seat, and when it's their turn, they just quietly sit in their seat at the table and receive the appreciation being expressed to them from others in the group.

To set this up, it's important to talk about the power of appreciation, and specifically the distinction between recognition and appreciation. It's also good to set some context for the exercise to let people know the reasons you are doing this: to have an opportunity to express and receive appreciation, to let people know what we value about them, and to enhance the level of caring and connection on the team.

Set a timer for two minutes and pick someone to go first (ideally, this is someone you think will be open and willing to authentically receive appreciation from others on the team without getting too uncomfortable about it or turning it into a joke). For those two minutes, everyone focuses their attention on the one person in the Appreciation Seat. In no particular order, anyone who feels moved to express their appreciation for this individual can do so.

The person receiving appreciation, can only say "Thank you." It's important to remind them (and everyone participating) about that, because there is often a tendency to deflect the appreciation being offered, mainly due to social norms, discomfort, or both. Not everyone has to say something, and usually there isn't even enough time for every member of the group to express their appreciation for this individual before the timer goes off (although if you have the time, go for it).

Once the two-minute timer goes off, continue going counterclockwise around the group until everyone has had a chance to be in the Appreciation Seat.

When the exercise ends and everyone has had a chance to be appreciated, thank the group. Then, ask them to reflect on their personal experience of being in the Appreciation Seat and doing the exercise together. It's also good to have a discussion about the power of appreciation in general and, more specifically, what your team can do to operate and communicate this way on an ongoing basis.

Even though most people acknowledge it can be a little awkward and vulnerable, especially at first, to receive appreciation from their teammates, it's usually incredibly valuable and powerful as well. It feels really good to be able to express appreciation for the people on their team and for it to be genuinely received.

The Impact of Appreciation

One of the specific interpersonal reasons that expressing appreciation can be challenging is that most of us aren't all that comfortable with *receiving* appreciation from others. We often feel uncomfortable when someone appreciates us, and as a social-norm reaction we tend either to give them a compliment right back or to deflect their appreciation with self-deprecation, self-criticism, or humor. While these reactions are normal, they get in the way of our ability to really take in the appreciation, and thus make it harder for people to express it to us.

Getting a compliment is like being given a gift: Our job is to receive it graciously and gratefully, not to give a quick gift back or somehow diminish it, which unfortunately is what we do much of the time. In the Appreciation Seat exercise, I remind everyone of these things and encourage them to listen, breathe, and really take in the appreciation that's being offered to them. It's not uncommon in this process for people to get emotional as they express and receive appreciation. It never ceases to amaze me how simple yet profound this can be.

I often wrap up the discussion following the Appreciation Seat exercise by reminding the group that, on the one hand, what we just did was forced and artificial: I told them to say positive things to each other and they did that. But given that they know each other, work together, and care about each other, finding things to appreciate about one another is usually easy and quite fulfilling; it just takes awareness, commitment, and courage. And even when it's "forced" like this, it can still be meaningful and genuine. I also let them know that they probably won't forget anytime soon what their teammates said to and about them. Finally, I encourage them to find simple and practical ways to express appreciation for one another (and for others, such as cross-functional partners, clients, senior leaders, and even friends and family) on a more regular basis. Appreciation has impact, and it's one of the most important aspects of showing people we care about them. Ultimately, it's one of the best things we can do to enhance the connection, culture, and performance of our team.

Curiosity and Interest

A basic yet really important aspect of caring about the people on our team (and anyone, for that matter) is being genuinely curious and interested in who they are and what makes them tick. A simple Google search of the word *caring* comes back with the definition, "displaying kindness and concern for others."

Roxanne Bisby Davis is the director of team analytics and research at Cisco. She's part of an organization at Cisco called Leadership and Team Intelligence that focuses on enabling the company's leaders and teams to perform at the highest level. By researching what the best managers and groups do specifically, Roxanne and her team are able to provide proven strategies and practical suggestions to their colleagues across Cisco in a way that helps them build high-performing team cultures.

Roxanne said, "Giving your attention to the people on your team is essential to the team's success. However, it's not attention in the way of having a few meetings now and then, a once-a-year retreat, or a monthly all-hands where you talk about strategy. It's the type of attention that allows you to learn about one another. It's understanding what makes each of you excited about your work, as well as what might bring you down. And it's the type of attention that is given often and consistently, having frequent opportunities throughout your days or weeks to connect."

She went on to say, "When this type of consistent and genuine interest is paid, what we have discovered is that those individuals, leaders, and teams that embrace seeking and giving attention are more highly engaged and have better performance than those who don't. We've also learned that these same people talk about work differently, in a more positive tone. And that when challenged to be their best every day by someone who knows and cares about them, they grow at faster rates."

Being curious about and interested in our teammates does take a certain amount of time and commitment. It's about a willingness to connect, engage, and get to know the people with whom we work on a human level. We may or may not have a lot in common with them, or even work and live in the same location. However, when we take the time to reach out, listen, ask questions, and genuinely pay attention to the people on our team, not only does it allow us to build stronger relationships with them personally, it also allows them, us, and everyone on the team to operate at a deeper and more successful level.

Compassion and Kindness

I've heard compassion described as "empathy in action." While empathy is about understanding and feeling the emotions of others, compassion is about wanting to contribute to their happiness and well-being. Compassion, therefore, is more proactive, which means we can make a habit of it. Teams that intentionally and habitually show compassion to one another are more connected and successful. In operating with compassion, we're demonstrating our care for each other in a specific, overt, and powerful way.

In an interview for *Psychology Today* in April 2018, Chris Kukk, professor of political and social science at Western Connecticut State University and author of *The Compassionate Achiever*, said, "Success is often associated with the individualistic idea of only looking out for number one. However, even Darwin suggested that the most efficient and effective species have the highest number of sympathetic members." According to Kukk's research, compassion helps build resilience, improve physical health, and is a consistent characteristic of success—individually and collectively. Teams that create a culture of compassion are more likely to be engaged, innovative, and collaborative with one another, and to perform at their best.

I had a chance to interview Scott Shute on my podcast. Scott was the VP of global customer operations at LinkedIn for six years—leading an organization of 1,000 people. His interest in leadership, culture, and performance led him to take on a new role in 2018 as the head of mindfulness and compassion programs. Scott and his team have implemented programs to support the people, leaders, and groups at LinkedIn to expand their awareness and skills. "One of the biggest skills needed to achieve our vision at LinkedIn is compassion," he said. "We believe that compassion is not just a better way to live, it's a better way to build a team and grow a business that is successful, sustainable, and has a positive impact in the world."

Kindness, like compassion, is something we can cultivate, nurture, and practice. Different from being "nice," which we previously discussed, being kind is about consciously and authentically choosing to be friendly, supportive, generous, and considerate toward our teammates (and everyone else we work and interact with). According to a study conducted by the American Psychological Association, people who were treated kindly at work repaid it by being 278 percent more generous to co-workers compared to a control group.

The great thing about both kindness and compassion is that they're contagious. The more willing we are to be compassionate and kind to our fellow team members, the more likely they are to be that way with us and everyone else on the team. And, as we consistently and deliberately practice compassion and kindness with the people on our team, we demonstrate our care for them and contribute to a culture that can allow us all to achieve our best results.

Balance

Being able to balance caring about and challenging the people on our team is not that easy, as I previously mentioned, yet it's fundamental to the culture and success of our group and organization. Dheeraj Pandey is the co-founder, chairman, and CEO of Nutanix, an enterprise software company based in San Jose, California, that helps organizations of all sizes modernize their datacenters and run applications, on-site or in the cloud. Nutanix was founded in 2009, went public in 2016, and in 2018 did more than $1 billion in revenue. The company has more than 5,000 employees and continues to grow. I've had the honor of partnering with Dheeraj, his leadership team, and their company over the past four years. It has been fun to see their remarkable growth. Dheeraj is a leader who combines an incredibly high IQ with an equally high EQ, which is one of the reasons he and his team have been so successful. He understands the importance of caring about and challenging people at the same time.

When I asked him about it, he told me, "Caring about and challenging our team means walking the tightrope, and balance is key. I constantly remind myself that long-term performance is about striking a balance between the head and the heart. In my company-building lessons, I've learned to appreciate the difference between what it means to be 'liked' vs. 'respected.'"

He went on to say, "Caring about people provides me the human currency to challenge them to think differently. One positive side effect of challenging our team is that it makes me think hard. There's a hidden vulnerability that drives me to read, consult experts, dig into history for parallels, and write when I'm challenging my team. That vulnerability—of not 'throwing my CEO badge' during those tough times—is another way to show them that I care. More important, it helps me refine my own thinking along the way, which is a powerful self-improvement technique, and ultimately, I hope, makes me and us better in the process."

This notion of balancing our head and our heart that Dheeraj mentioned is so important, as well as understanding that our ability to genuinely care about people gives us the "currency" or permission to be able to challenge them in a way that they might listen to, be inspired by, and allow to impact them positively.

If we care about people but don't challenge them, they may feel nurtured and connected to us and the team, but they won't be pushed to be their best and reach their full potential individually, and we won't be able to thrive collectively. If we challenge people but don't genuinely care about them, they might be motivated to work hard and produce results initially, but over time they will get stressed out, burned out, and become resentful.

We have to be able to do both of these things passionately, authentically, and with a healthy balance.

Commitment

Commitment is fundamental to the culture of our team and our ability to perform at the highest level.

Legendary football coach Vince Lombardi, who led the Green Bay Packers to the first two Super Bowl victories in NFL history said, "Individual commitment to a group effort: That is what makes a team work, a company work, a society work, a civilization work."

And while Lombardi was right and knew a thing or two about team performance, in addition to the individuals on our team making a commitment to our collective effort, we also have to be clear on our goals, pledge ourselves to them, and commit to each other.

I sometimes ask people at the beginning of team-development programs I deliver to think of the best teams they've been on over the course of their lives and to reflect on the qualities that made those teams great. While I hear lots of different things in response to this question, the themes of commitment and "having each other's backs" are ones that come up all the time.

When we commit to a clear goal or set of goals that are bigger than we are personally and inspire us collectively, it can challenge us to come together and do extraordinary things. According to author Neil Kokemuller, "The major benefit of team commitment is improved bottom line results. Committed employees make decisions that benefit their colleagues, team, and organization. Collaboration on projects and work usually leads to better ideas and more effective performance."

In order to collaborate in a way that brings out the best in all of us, we need to commit fully to what we're doing and to each other. This doesn't mean we're perfect, we never make mistakes, we don't have doubts, or that we agree with each other all the time. As we've discussed throughout the book, great teams allow each other to mess up, do whatever they can to create a sense of belonging,

WE'RE ALL IN THIS TOGETHER

and lean into the discomfort of conflict and feedback. All of these things, and others, that are necessary for team success can be daunting and uncomfortable. To move through our fear and discomfort, there has to be something big and important that we're striving for.

Committing to each other and to the team means that we can count on one another to bring our best, to do what we say we're going to do by when we say we're going to do it, and that we're invested in each other's success and well-being. For our team to perform in the way we truly want it to, we have to be all in on what we're doing, our goals, and each other.

Accountability

Commitment and accountability are directly linked. Accountability, however, is somewhat similar to conflict and feedback in that it's necessary for growth, development, performance, and success, yet it's often challenging and uncomfortable. Most of us don't like being held accountable, and we really don't like holding others accountable. However, lack of accountability is detrimental to our success—individually and collectively.

Mike Thaman, chairman and former CEO of Owens Corning, makes a critical distinction between "holding someone accountable," which has mainly negative and punitive connotations, and "creating accountability in others," which is about being vested in the performance and success of people.

Having psychological safety, a sense of real belonging, and a willingness to have those sweaty-palmed conversations on our team are all important to creating this type of healthy accountability. It's also essential to have clear goals that we're focused on and standards by which we expect our teammates and ourselves to operate. Committing to these goals and standards, and creating a culture of accountability among our teammates, supports the execution and performance of everyone on the team and our team as a whole.

Joel Constable is the director of talent development at Intuit. He and I have known each other and partnered a number of times in the past when he worked at both Google and Pinterest. When I asked Joel specifically about how teams can get better at creating accountability, he said, "One of the most effective practices I've seen is ensuring consistent clarity and alignment of commitments. Even teams with strong trust can struggle with accountability if they haven't taken the time to get crystal clear, in writing, what each person is committing to and by when. I may feel comfortable holding a teammate accountable when they miss a deliverable, but if they had a different understanding of the deliverable or timeline, accountability becomes much more challenging."

He went on to say, "Ambiguity is often the enemy of accountability. I find that this is also a common mistake in meetings—actions are discussed and there is a loose understanding of who should do what, but teams don't take adequate time to clearly align on owners and deadlines. However, when this does happen, it makes not only accountability easier, it's much more likely that these things will get done."

The clearer we are about what we specifically intend to do or accomplish, and by when, the more likely we can be supported and held accountable by our teammates, and the better we'll be at holding them and ourselves accountable as well. The stronger and healthier the accountability is on our team, the better we can perform.

My friend and colleague Anese Cavanaugh, author of *Contagious Culture*, told me "The best teams I work with create agreements with each other for how they want to be held accountable and push each other." In other words, they take ownership for their success and solicit the support and accountability from their teammates in specific ways that they know will enhance their performance, and that of the team.

Accountability isn't about shame, blame, or judgment—all of which are detrimental to our relationships, culture, and ability to perform, by the way. It's about committing to goals, to standards of behavior, and to specific actions, knowing that our team is paying attention, cares about us, and is invested in our individual and collective success enough to hold us to these things.

Grit

The concept of grit has always been important for individual and team success. We've been talking about it a lot more in the past few years, thanks, in part, to the research of Angela Duckworth, a professor of psychology at the University of Pennsylvania, and her best-selling book, *Grit: The Power of Passion and Perseverance*, which came out in 2016. According to Duckworth and her extensive research, grit is the ability to stick with things over the long haul until you master them, even and especially when there are setbacks along the way. She says, "The gritty individual approaches achievement as a marathon; his or her advantage is stamina."

While we often focus on the importance of grit for individual development, performance, and success, it's also essential for teams. In a piece for the *Harvard*

Business Review published in the fall 2018, Duckworth and Thomas Lee, a professor at Harvard Medical School, write, "Gritty teams collectively have the same traits that gritty individuals do: a desire to work hard, learn, and improve; resilience in the face of setbacks; and a strong sense of priorities and purpose."

Even though the pace of business and change today is quite rapid, grit is essential for our team to succeed over a sustained period of time. There are going to be ups and downs, wins and losses, and lots of adversity to overcome. We have to be able to focus on the long-term goals we have both individually and collectively if we're going to have the stamina to dig deep and do great work over a significant period of time.

Bringing Out the Best in Your Team

Teams that perform at the highest level know how to bring out the best in each other. They care enough about one another and are so committed to their collective success, that they have permission to challenge each other—knowing that doing so allows everyone to fulfill their potential. It can look lots of different ways, but the underlying awareness is that for each individual on the team and the team as a whole to be the very best it can be, they need to be able to push each other to tap into their collective greatness.

When Draymond Green of the Golden State Warriors gets into the faces of his teammates and screams at them on the basketball court, as he sometimes does, he's doing that because he's committed to the success of the team and to his teammates. He's able to do it because his fellow players know how much he cares about them and wants to win.

The Warriors have created an incredibly high standard of excellence that Draymond and his teammates are committed to, and he knows that his job is help the team win—both with his play on the court and his willingness to challenge his teammates to be their absolute best.

We may or may not have the type of personality that lends itself to us getting into the faces of our teammates. Based on the culture of our team and the specific people on it, that may not even be the best approach. However, figuring out ways to get the most out of each other and being willing to push one another are critical aspects of team performance and success.

We all want to be challenged in ways that bring out the best in us and those around us. It takes courage and commitment to interact this way, but it's definitely worth it and is necessary to our relationships, performance, and culture on so many levels. Great teams, just like great families, know that in order to function in the healthiest and most productive way possible, it's essential to care about and challenge one another at the same time.

The Leader's Role in Caring About and Challenging Each Other

Leaders set the tone for their teams. When it comes to caring about and challenging each other, it's critical for leaders to do both of these things passionately and with balance, as we've discussed in various ways throughout this chapter. Here are some specific things you can think about and do as a leader to impact the performance of your team along these lines.

Appreciate the people on the team. When I interviewed Keith White, EVP of loss prevention and global sustainability at Gap Inc., on my podcast he said, "Great leaders love people." He's right. This doesn't mean you have to be best friends with everyone on your team, but it does mean that you love coaching people, helping them, and doing everything you can to support their success. One of the most powerful ways to do this is to appreciate them, which means continually recognizing their value as human beings, not just acknowledging their skills, results, or accomplishments. Look for ways to express your appreciation—in meetings, conversations, e-mails, and more. You can facilitate the Appreciation Seat exercise that I wrote about on pages 136–138 at team meetings or offsites. And you can simply listen and pay attention to what matters to the people on your team. Everyone wants to be seen, heard, and to know that who they are is important to you as their leader and to the success of the team. Appreciation allows this to happen, and when it's expressed authentically, it can have a huge impact.

Set clear expectations. Clarity is essential for success. If you want your team members and the team as a whole to perform at a high level, it's critical for you to let them know exactly what you expect. When people know what great looks like, they can aim for it. Setting clear expectations is about having a healthy high bar. When the expectations are clear, creating accountability becomes much easier for you as a leader and for the team as a whole. Letting people know what you want and expect from them makes it much more likely that they can achieve it, and it eliminates a lot of confusion, ambiguity, and struggle. Through its Project Aristotle study, which we talked about in Pillar #1,

WE'RE ALL IN THIS TOGETHER

Google discovered not only how important psychological safety is to the success and performance of a team, it also determined that structure and clarity are essential as well.

When goals, roles, and execution plans are clear, the team can thrive. One of your main responsibilities as a leader is to make sure there is clarity on these things for everyone on the team.

Know what motivates people and what stresses them out. To inspire the performance of the people on your team and help the team win, it's important to know as much as you can about your team members. A great conversation you can have with each of your direct reports, and even with the team as a whole, can start like this: "If I want to motivate and inspire you, what are some specific things I can do and say to help make that happen? And, on the flip side, if I were to irritate, annoy, and stress you out, what would that look like?" In other words, have a conversation with everyone on your team so that you know explicitly from them what motivates them and what stresses them out. This awareness can help inform how you communicate with and coach them, and will also let them know how committed you are to being the best possible leader for them and the team.

Push people out of their comfort zone. I love this quote from author Neale Donald Walsch: "Life begins at the end of your comfort zone." It's so true. Where real growth and performance happens is beyond our comfort zone. However, because this can be scary and uncomfortable, we need people around us to care about and challenge us. As a leader, one of the most important things you can do to support the growth and success of the people around you and your team is to push them past their perceived limits. You need to first care about and appreciate them and also have their permission. Assuming those things are in place, your ability and willingness to challenge them passionately is fundamental to their performance. Challenging them with specific requests, and creating accountability so that they're compelled to take risks, try new things, and take ownership of their progress are all things that will serve them and ultimately the team as well.

Create accountability for *yourself* with the team. In your role you most likely have some accountability with the person you report to, as well as the team you're a member of (your first team). You also have a critical role in the accountability of the team that reports to you (your second team) and each of its members. However, to really create a strong culture of commitment and performance, you must also create accountability for yourself with them. In other words, be clear about the goals, standards, and actions you commit to and hold yourself accountable with your direct reports for those things specifically. This means doing what you say you're going to do and operating by the values and standards you set for yourself and the team (and, when this doesn't happen, owning up to it and making things right).

Your willingness to hold yourself accountable will set the tone for the team and allow them to hold themselves and each other accountable in a healthy way that drives performance all the way around.

The Team Member's Role in Caring About and Challenging Each Other

Your ability to care about and challenge your peers has so much to do with the culture of your team and how you're able to perform—personally and collectively. Many of the things just mentioned about what leaders can do also apply to team members.

Here are some additional things for you to think about and do to ensure that the people on your team are cared about and challenged in a way that will help them and your entire group succeed.

Appreciate your peers. Let your teammates know what you admire about them, value in them, and want to thank them for. This goes a long way toward building trust and connection, and makes them more open to your feedback, support, and challenge. It's also important to include your manager and others (cross-functional partners, senior leaders, external partners, and anyone else you work with) in your appreciation. When you let people know the positive impact they have on you, they feel seen, valued, and cared about. Send notes of appreciation and copy others. Express appreciation at the start and end of meetings. Ask your manager to do the Appreciation Seat exercise at offsites. Find ways, both big and small, to express your appreciation for the people around you.

Let people know what motivates you and what stresses you out. Similar to the conversation I suggested that leaders have with their direct reports, you can take it upon yourself to have that same conversation with your own manager, or anyone else you work with. You can say, "Do you want to get the most out of me and have me be incredibly motivated and inspired? Here's how you can do that . . . " And then let them know specifically what you want. Additionally, you can say, "If you want to stress me out, shut me down, and really irritate me, here's how you can do that . . . " The more specific you are about this, the better. Having the self-awareness and courage to share these requests and insights authentically with your manager, teammates, and others will allow you to deepen your relationships with them, give them important perspective on how to best motivate and communicate with you, and open up a dialogue of support and partnership that can benefit each of you and the entire team.

Proactively create accountability. Because accountability can be scary and stressful on both sides of the equation, creating it for ourselves in a proactive way is one of the best approaches we can take. This means asking our manager and teammates to hold us accountable in a way that supports our growth and success. It also means taking ownership to hold ourselves accountable. For example, if you know there are certain tasks or goals that are challenging for you, when you meet with your manager one-on-one, make specific commitments about what you will do or accomplish over the next week (or month, or quarter) and use the structure of your regular meetings to check back in about those things—to make sure you're making progress or to get specific support if you're struggling. The more proactive we are with accountability the less stressful it will be, and the more we can influence a culture of commitment and accountability on our team.

Commit to the team. For you to be the best team player possible and for your team to succeed at the highest level, you and your teammates have to be all in. This requires your commitment. Commitment doesn't mean we agree with everything that is happening 100 percent, or that everyone on the team is our best friend. Commitment is about fully buying in to the goals, values, culture, and people on the team. It's about having everyone's backs and doing whatever it takes to ensure the team's success. It's also remembering that our primary job is to help the team win and making sure we deal with anything that gets in the way of our success. The word *commitment* means "the state or quality of being dedicated to a cause or activity." Committing yourself to the team means being fully dedicated to the "cause" that you and your teammates are focused on accomplishing.

Root for your teammates. Great teams root for each other. Some of my favorite examples of this in recent years, as I've touched on a few times already, come from watching the Golden State Warriors play basketball—especially when their starters are on the bench. The way they root for their teammates with such joy and passion is a sign of their strong culture and the commitment they have to one another's success. Remembering that performance is contagious, rooting for our teammates is both about celebrating them when they succeed and creating a culture of excellence for our team. It's a practical way to embody the idea that we're all in this together. Get excited about the skills, execution, and performance of your teammates and let them know. This will not only have them feel cared about and valued, it will motivate them to continue to work hard and succeed, and will also inspire you and everyone else on the team.

What Your Team Can Do Together to Care About and Challenge Each Other

In addition to the things that leaders and team members can do individually, here are some things to think about and act upon as a team to make sure we collectively care about and challenge one another:

Be invested in each other. Caring about one another is all about being invested in each other. This means that we take interest in our teammates, get to know one another personally, and commit to supporting the people on our team to be as successful as they can be—at work and in life. Be curious about your teammates, find out what they value, and be willing to support them in any way you can. When teams are invested in one another personally, they take pride in helping each other out and sharing in everyone's success, which allows them to produce extraordinary results together.

Create team rituals. Rituals are an essential aspect of high-performing teams. They can be as simple as when and how often you meet as a team and one-on-one, what people do with their laptops and phones during meetings, having regular check-ins, how you regularly connect with people on the team who work in different locations, eating or taking breaks together, huddling up during the day or week if you can, and more. These and so many other things can be ritualized by your team.

Roxanne Bisby Davis from Cisco, whom I quoted earlier in this chapter, said this about the power of rituals, "When your team has established rituals, meaning the repeated actions that define what matters most to the team, they hold everyone accountable for a particular way of working.

These rituals are also an anchor when someone new joins to bring them into the squad. When you're clear about what you stand for and the way that you work together, it doesn't leave anything up for interpretation and allows for excellence to prevail, even in the tough times."

Some rituals may be initiated and facilitated by the leader, but it's best when the team can create and commit to these as a group—taking ownership and having accountability for them collectively.

Set clear standards. Similar to rituals, setting clear standards by which your team operates is important. These standards make it clear what we expect from each other and ourselves, in terms of behavior, communication, attendance, engagement, deliverables, and more. From preparing for meetings, to dealing with disagreements, to managing deadlines, to communicating with one another, the clearer the team is about the standards by which you all agree to operate, the better you'll be able to align, collaborate, and perform together.

Take collective responsibility. One of the best lessons I learned as an athlete was that you win and lose as a team. Of course, there are usually key contributions from specific individuals that impact the outcome more than others, but when a team operates with collective responsibility they support each other in a way that serves the success of the team in the best way possible. As the cliché goes, "There's no 'I' in team." And, as soccer legend Mia Hamm said, "I am a member of a team, and I rely on the team, I defer to it and sacrifice for it, because the team, not the individual, is the ultimate champion."

Taking collective responsibility is about creating a culture of accountability where the entire team adopts a mindset of ownership and each member does everything he or she can to help the team succeed, which is the ultimate goal.

Celebrate together. One of the most exciting aspects of being on a team is having a chance to celebrate with our teammates. In sports, one of the best parts of winning a big game or a championship is the postgame (or postseason) celebration. In life and in business, there aren't always big "games" that we either win or lose. So, what great teams have to learn to do is to celebrate the milestones and successes along the way, and find ways to celebrate the effort, commitment, and sacrifice involved in the work. Due to the pace and nature of business today, this isn't always easy to do, but it's necessary. Teams that have fun and that make a commitment to play and celebrate together build strong bonds, and in doing so they inspire themselves to even greater success.

This fourth and final pillar is the culmination of what we've been discussing throughout the book. When we create psychological safety, make sure people are included and feel that they belong, and have the courage to embrace those important sweaty-palmed conversations, we set ourselves up to be able to care about and challenge each other in an authentic and important way. And when we do all four of these things, we remember that we're truly all in this together, and we can create a team culture of high performance, trust, and belonging, which is what we all want and what allows us to thrive.

CONCLUSION

About six years ago I was sitting in a hotel conference room in Switzerland with a senior leadership team from Roche. They were having a multiday offsite and they'd invited me to deliver a daylong team development program. I was excited to be there, but was feeling exhausted and emotional. It was my third international trip in just two months, and due to my jet lag, I'd gotten less than an hour of sleep the night before. My sister Lori, who had been diagnosed with cancer two years earlier but had been in remission for the past year, just found out that her cancer had returned, which was scary, sad, and daunting.

Even with all of this going on, I was doing my best to focus on the team and the session. They were a really good group—super smart, engaged, and interesting—and had been performing pretty well but were working through some challenges. They also had to navigate the complex dynamics of leading a global organization with some members living in Switzerland and working out of the Roche office in Basel, others living in the Bay Area near me and working out of the Genentech office (a subsidiary of Roche), while still others lived and worked elsewhere in the world.

As we moved through the session, we got to the point in the program where I was setting up the "If you really knew me . . . " exercise. Maybe it was because I was feeling so tired and raw, or because I knew this team was specifically responsible for the development and distribution of

WE'RE ALL IN THIS TOGETHER

cancer medications like the ones Lori was about to start taking again, but as I began the exercise and lowered the waterline on my own iceberg, I got quite emotional talking about her and how I was feeling in that moment. I could tell that a number of people could relate, and I felt a lot of empathy from the group.

As we went around and each person shared what was going on for them, there was a lot of emotion in the room. Some people shared about having family members who were dealing with illnesses like Lori's, others talked about parents who were aging, some shared about children who were growing up, and others addressed stresses at work, as well as fears about the future, difficulty balancing personal and professional commitments, painful losses, leadership challenges, dreams, and more. While everyone talked about their own life and their unique experiences and feelings, there was something universal about what we all shared: We were telling the truth about being human. It went quite deep and there were lots of tears.

As we were wrapping up the exercise, a man raised his hand. He was one of the people on the team who seemed a bit shy and reserved. I was intrigued by what he wanted to say, so I called on him. "Wow," he said, "that was intense. But I really appreciated how open, real, and vulnerable everyone was. Thank you." He then asked quietly, his voice shaking a bit with emotion, "Mike, I wonder if we can take a break now and just go around and give each other some hugs?" I smiled and said, "Of course."

For the next 15 minutes this team of incredibly educated, skilled, and accomplished senior leaders walked around that room hugging, crying, and laughing with one another. It wasn't about titles, roles, backgrounds, goals, results, market conditions, strategies, plans, objectives, or anything else. It was about a group of human beings who work really hard together and care about each other, sharing their truth and their humanity, and connecting on a human level. It was beautiful, and I was honored to be there with them in that experience.

Coming together as a team isn't easy, as we've discussed throughout this book. We all bring baggage and expectations from our family and our previous experiences with us. There are lots of factors, influences, fears, and dynamics that make it hard, especially these days. And as we listen to the news and pay attention to what's going on in the country and the world right now, it's easy to feel discouraged, disconnected, and to buy in to the negativity and division. We can get so caught up in the intense pace and pressure that we lose sight of how important the people around us are.

However, as I've seen over the course of my life and through my experience working with people, teams, and organizations of all kinds over the past few decades, we're hardwired for connection and we want to come together. Even and especially in the midst of the diversity and complexity of today's world, we know deep down that we belong to each other, that we're way more alike than we are different, and that we truly need one another.

We can never know exactly what the future holds—where our careers will take us, how our teams will perform, what will happen with our companies, where the economy will go, who the president or leaders of our country will be, how things will turn out for our loved ones or just about anything else—big or small. My sister Lori died a little over a year after that meeting I attended in Switzerland. And while that was an incredibly painful experience, the empathy and kindness I received from the Roche team that day was real, as was all the love and support I got from my family, friends, colleagues, and clients during

WE'RE ALL IN THIS TOGETHER

that difficult time. Having experienced quite a bit of loss and grief in my life, I know it's hard, but it's also one of the most universal human experiences we have. And in order to get through it and heal, we have to lean on those around us.

The truth is that life and business always have been, and always will be, uncertain. And while this can be terrifying, it's also just the nature of things, and the fundamental vulnerability of being human. Are there issues and challenges facing us societally, organizationally, and personally? Of course. Do we have our work cut out for us? Definitely. Can we rise up and meet these challenges? For sure.

But to do so in the way that's necessary right now, as well as for us to do our best work, have the kind of impact we truly want to have, and unlock our full potential, we can't do it alone; we must do it together.

If you and your team are willing to do what it takes, even in the face of resistance, doubt, and cynicism—to create psychological safety, to focus on inclusion and belonging, to embrace sweaty-palmed conversations, and to care about and challenge each other—you can build and sustain an incredibly strong culture of trust and performance, and accomplish remarkable things.

Doing this requires willingness, commitment, and courage. And, most important, a deep understanding that there really isn't a *them*, it's all *us,* and we truly are all in this together!

RESOURCES

Below you'll find a list of books, workshops, podcasts, conferences, videos, and more. All of these resources are ones that I believe in and recommend strongly. Each will support and empower you on your path of growth and discovery, and can also help those around you and your team.

From Me

Be Yourself, Everyone Else Is Already Taken (book)
Bring Your Whole Self to Work (book)
Focus on the Good Stuff (book)
Nothing Changes Until You Do (book)
"The Power of Appreciation" (audio)
TED talks (videos) – Mike-Robbins.com/Videos
We're All in This Together (podcast) – Mike-Robbins.com/Podcasts

Books

Conscious Capitalism, by John Mackey and Raj Sisodia
The Culture Code, by Daniel Coyle
Dare to Lead, by Brené Brown
Delivering Happiness, by Tony Hsieh
Don't Sweat the Small Stuff at Work, by Richard Carlson
Drive, by Daniel Pink
Emotional Intelligence, by Daniel Goleman

The Fearless Organization, by Amy Edmondson
Find Your Why, by Simon Sinek
The Five Dysfunctions of a Team, by Patrick Lencioni
Great Teams, by Don Yaeger
Grit, by Angela Duckworth
How to Be an Inclusive Leader, by Jennifer Brown
Leading with Cultural Intelligence, by David Livermore
Leading with Noble Purpose, by Lisa Earle McLeod
Lean In, by Sheryl Sandberg
Mindset, by Carol Dweck
No Hard Feelings, by Liz Fosslien and Mollie West Duffy
Option B, Sheryl Sandberg and Adam Grant
Peak, by Chip Conley
The Power of a Positive Team, by Jon Gordon
Radical Candor, by Kim Scott
Rising Strong, by Brené Brown
Search Inside Yourself, by Chade-Meng Tan
Social Intelligence, by Daniel Goleman
StandOut 2.0, by Marcus Buckingham
Start Something That Matters, by Blake Mycoskie
StrengthsFinder 2.0, by Tom Rath
Success Intelligence, by Robert Holden
Team Human, by Douglas Rushkoff
Teaming, by Amy Edmondson
Thrive, by Arianna Huffington
Triggers, by Marshall Goldsmith
The Way We're Working Isn't Working, by Tony Schwartz
White Fragility, by Robin DiAngelo
Wolfpack, Abby Wambach
Work Rules!, by Laszlo Bock
You Win in the Locker Room First, by Jon Gordon
and Mike Smith

Workshops

Being the Change (ChallengeDay.org)
The Hoffman Process (HoffmanInstitute.org)
The Landmark Forum (LandmarkWorldwide.com)
The New Warrior Training Adventure (ManKindProject.org)
The Shadow Process (TheFordInstitute.com)

Podcasts

Ten Percent Happier with Dan Harris
Armchair Expert with Dax Shepard
Good Life Project with Jonathan Fields
HBR IdeaCast
The Marie Forleo Podcast
The School of Greatness with Lewis Howes
The TED Radio Hour from NPR
The Tim Ferriss Show
WTF with Marc Maron

Conferences/Retreat Centers

1440 Multiversity (1440.org)
Better Man Conference (BetterManConference.com)
Conscious Capitalism Conference (ConsciousCapitalism
.org)
Culture First Conference (CultureAmp.com)
Esalen Institute (Esalen.org)
Omega Institute (Eomega.org)
South by Southwest (SXSW.com)
Wisdom 2.0 Conference (Wisdom2Summit.com)
Workhuman Live (Workhuman.com)

Videos/Websites/Blogs

The Call to Courage (Brené Brown on Netflix)
HBR.org (Harvard Business Review website)
Forbes.com (*Forbes* magazine website)
The Mask You Live In (TheRepresentationProject.org)
TED.com (any and all videos on this site or app, especially by Brené Brown, Daniel Pink, Elizabeth Gilbert, Simon Sinek, and Steve Jobs)

ACKNOWLEDGMENTS

I am so grateful to the wonderful people who supported me in making this book a reality and who support me in my work and my life. First and most important, Michelle Benoit Robbins, I love and adore you! Thank you for your incredible generosity, love, support, understanding, and kindness. You are amazing and I could not have written this book, do the work that I do, or be the man that I am without the remarkable way you love, encourage, and hold space for me. Samantha Benoit Robbins, I love being your dad and appreciate the passion, curiosity, and thoughtfulness you bring to the world and my life. Thank you for all the ways you continue to teach me. Annarose Benoit Robbins, thank you for your humor, wisdom, and the way you challenge yourself, me, and everyone to bring it. I love watching you grow and learning from you. Rachel Cohen, thank you for being such a great sister and friend, and thanks for your inspiration and your love.

Melanie Bates, you have been and continue to be such a gift in my life. Thank you for your remarkable coaching, editing, and partnership on this book. I'm grateful for our friendship, and for how you share your gifts and talents with me.

Michele Martin and Steve Harris, thank you for your continued support and belief in me and my work. I'm grateful to have you as agents and as part of our team. Meredith Reese, you're such a gamer. Thanks for your extraordinary commitment, passion, and enthusiasm, and for all the wonderful ways you support me, our team, and

169

our vision. Lorrin Maughan, you were such a joy to work with on this project. Your great research and enthusiasm had an incredibly positive impact on this book and on me, thank you. Andrew Deutscher, thank you for your belief in me and my work, for your partnership, and for all the ways you continue to challenge and support the growth of our business.

Reid Tracy, Patty Gift, Sally Mason-Swaab, Lindsay McGinty, and the entire Hay House team—thank you for your continued partnership and support. I'm grateful to be a part of the Hay House family.

Kalyn Cai Bennett, I appreciate your wonderful work and the way you have supported me to be healthy, inspired, and aligned for the past number of years. Eleanor, thank you for your wisdom and guidance. You continue to inspire me to change, grow, and stretch in positive ways that I truly appreciate.

I'm grateful to Eric Severson, Chip Conley, Keith White, Kim Scott, Jennifer Brown, Karen May, Aimée Lapic, Roxanne Bisby Davis, Dan Henkle, Robert Holden, Scott Shute, Jason and Shay Hughes, Anese Cavanaugh, Joel Constable, Rich and Yvonne Dutra-St. John, Nilofer Merchant, Andrea Hough, Dheeraj Pandey, Nate Regier, and all the other wonderful people who have contributed their stories, wisdom, and ideas to this book. Thank you!

Brené Brown, Glennon Doyle, Elizabeth Gilbert, Sheryl Sandberg, Simon Sinek, Marcus Buckingham, Daniel Goleman, Tom Rath, Amy Edmondson, Jon Gordon, Carol Dweck, and Angela Duckworth: Thank you for your inspiring work, which has had an impact on me personally, on my work, and, specifically, on this book.

To all of our clients, especially the ones who partner with us on a regular basis—Google, Wells Fargo, Deltek,

Schwab, Genentech, Nutanix, Hughes Marino, Microsoft, Pinterest, eBay, OneMain, Pandora, BioMarin, Houston Methodist, and Washington Speakers Bureau—thank you for your interest in my work and for trusting me to speak to and work with your people, leaders, and teams. I'm honored and grateful for our partnership.

To all the people who have come on my podcast as guests over the past few years, thank you for sharing your stories, insights, wisdom, and vulnerability with me and all of us.

To the wonderful staff at the Roman Spa in Calistoga, California: Thank you for taking such good care of me all the times I came to stay at your great property while I was writing this book (and my previous two books as well). I love it there and appreciate your service and support.

I'm also grateful to my family, friends, and all the people who support, inspire, and challenge me to be all I can be. Thanks for being there and reminding me that we truly are all in this together.

ABOUT THE AUTHOR

Mike Robbins is the author of *Bring Your Whole Self to Work; Nothing Changes Until You Do; Be Yourself, Everyone Else Is Already Taken;* and *Focus on the Good Stuff,* which have been translated into 15 languages. He's a sought-after speaker, consultant, and thought leader who delivers keynotes and seminars around the world. His clients include Google, Wells Fargo, Microsoft, Gap, Genentech, LinkedIn, Schwab, Airbnb, the NBA, eBay, Deloitte, Pinterest, the Oakland A's, Pandora, Nutanix, Deltek, and many others.

Prior to his current work, Mike was drafted by the New York Yankees out of high school, but chose instead to play baseball at Stanford University, where he pitched in the College World Series and earned his degree in American studies, with a specialization in race and ethnicity. After college, he played baseball professionally in the Kansas City Royals organization until an injury ended his career while he was still in the minor leagues. He then worked in sales and business development for two tech start-ups before starting his own consulting company in 2001.

Mike is a regular contributor to *Forbes* and the host of a weekly podcast called *We're All in This Together.* His work has been featured in *The Harvard Business Review, The New York Times, Fast Company, The Wall Street Journal,* and *The Economist,* as well as on NPR and ABC News, among many others. Mike lives in the San Francisco Bay Area with this wife, Michelle, and their two daughters, Samantha and Rosie.

To learn more about Mike and his work, visit Mike-Robbins .com, and connect with him on social media: LinkedIn (@MRobbins), Facebook (@MikeRobbinsPage), Twitter & Instagram (@MikeDRobbins).

Hay House Titles of Related Interest

THE SHIFT, the movie,
starring Dr. Wayne W. Dyer
(available as a 1-DVD program, an expanded
2-DVD set, and on online streaming video)
Watch the trailer at: www.hayhouse.com/the-shift-movie

∞

ASK: The Counterintuitive Online Method to Discover
Exactly *What Your Customers Want to Buy . . .*
Create a Mass of Raving Fans . . . and Take Any *Business to the*
Next Level, by Ryan Levesque

CHILLPRENEUR: The New Rules for Creating Success,
Freedom, and Abundance on Your Own Terms,
by Denise Duffield-Thomas

HIGH PERFORMANCE HABITS: How Extraordinary
People Become That Way, by Brendon Burchard

MILLIONAIRE SUCCESS HABITS:
The Gateway to Wealth & Prosperity, by Dean Graziosi

All of the above are available at your local
bookstore or may be ordered by visiting:

Hay House USA: www.hayhouse.com®
Hay House Australia: www.hayhouse.com.au
Hay House UK: www.hayhouse.co.uk
Hay House India: www.hayhouse.co.in

All of the above are available at your local bookstore,
or may be ordered by contacting Hay House (see next page).

∞

We hope you enjoyed this Hay House book. If you'd like to receive our online catalog featuring additional information on Hay House books and products, or if you'd like to find out more about the Hay Foundation, please contact:

Hay House, Inc., P.O. Box 5100, Carlsbad, CA 92018-5100
(760) 431-7695 or (800) 654-5126
(760) 431-6948 (fax) or (800) 650-5115 (fax)
www.hayhouse.com® • www.hayfoundation.org

———

Published in Australia by: Hay House Australia Pty. Ltd.,
18/36 Ralph St., Alexandria NSW 2015
Phone: 612-9669-4299 • *Fax:* 612-9669-4144
www.hayhouse.com.au

Published in the United Kingdom by: Hay House UK, Ltd.,
The Sixth Floor, Watson House, 54 Baker Street, London W1U 7BU
Phone: +44 (0)20 3927 7290 • *Fax:* +44 (0)20 3927 7291
www.hayhouse.co.uk

Published in India by: Hay House Publishers India,
Muskaan Complex, Plot No. 3, B-2, Vasant Kunj, New Delhi 110 070
Phone: 91-11-4176-1620 • *Fax:* 91-11-4176-1630
www.hayhouse.co.in

———

Access New Knowledge.
Anytime. Anywhere.

Learn and evolve at your own pace
with the world's leading experts.

www.hayhouseU.com

Listen. Learn. Transform.

Listen to the audio version of this book for FREE!

Today, life is more hectic than ever—so you deserve on-demand and on-the-go solutions that inspire growth, center your mind, and support your well-being.

Introducing the *Hay House Unlimited Audio* mobile app. Now you can listen to this book (and countless others)—without having to restructure your day.

With your membership, you can:

- Enjoy over 30,000 hours of audio from your favorite authors.
- Explore audiobooks, meditations, Hay House Radio episodes, podcasts, and more.
- Listen anytime and anywhere with offline listening.
- Access exclusive audios you won't find anywhere else.

Try FREE for 7 days!